AFRICAN
ANECDOTES

AFRICAN ANECDOTES

Reminiscences of a British Diplomat in Africa

By Peter Penfold

Front cover by an unknown Sierra Leone artist
on a mural at Moyamba Junction, Freetown-Bo
highway, in 2009, regrettably later destroyed.

Book design by Ben Greehy

I dedicate this book to all those, several mentioned in the book, who have enriched my life over these past many years, during my adventures in Africa. I acknowledge their contributions to the anecdotes I have related and I accept and apologise for any misrepresentations which are due to my ignorance and enthusiasm.

I want to thank my godson, Jack Latham, who kindly helped me self-publish the book through the services of Amazon and Kindle Direct Publishing.

All the photographs in the book are from my personal collection other than the photograph of Milton Obote and Idi Amin which came from the Ugandan Government Information Services.

Peter Penfold
Abingdon, Oxfordshire
2021

By the same author

Atrocities, Diamonds and Diplomacy –
The Inside Story of the Conflict in Sierra Leone
Published by Pen & Sword Books Ltd in UK 2012

and, with Barbara Davidson,

John-Abu Goes to School
Published by Mount Everest Publishing House Freetown Sierra Leone 2004

John-Abu Goes to Freetown
Published by Sierra Leone Writers Series Freetown Sierra Leone 2019

Contents

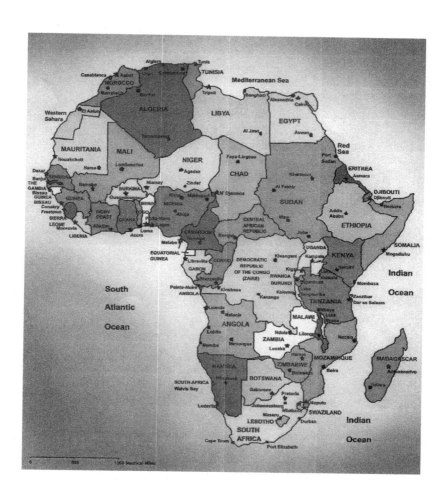

Introduction

When I first joined the Foreign Service in 1963, I had little idea of where my career would take me. After a couple of years in the Foreign Office in London as a grade 10 Clerical Officer, the lowest of the low, where one of my duties would be to ensure that the coal scuttle was filled with coal in order to heat the room in Winter, I received notification of my first overseas posting – the British Embassy, Bonn, West Germany. I was excited. Given I had a smattering of German (School A level) and it was in the centre of Western Europe and not that far from home, it was a very easy introduction to diplomatic life overseas. At that time Britain was making her first attempts to join the 'Common Market' which meant frequent visits to Bonn by Prime Minister Harold Wilson and his somewhat erratic Foreign Minister George Brown; so although I was only a lowly registry clerk in the Chancery, I felt that I was doing a worthwhile job in an important place.

Then after the regular two and a half years I received a phone call from the Personnel Department in London telling me to pack my effects and head for Kaduna. Kaduna – where was that? I had no idea. I discovered it was in Northern Nigeria. From being a member of the 100 strong British Embassy Bonn staff I would now be one of the 6 man staff of the Deputy British High Commission Kaduna, still a grade 10 registry officer.

In later years members of the Foreign Service were allowed to be much more choosy over where they went, but not at that time. I would never have dreamt of asking to go to Kaduna. I just had to go where I was told, and I was so glad I did. This started my relationship with Africa, an affair which proved to be for me so interesting and rewarding. They say that once you dip your toe into the Nile you will always return. Well Kaduna was far away from the

Nile, even from West Africa's mighty river, the Congo, but nonetheless, even though I had other postings around the world, notably in the Caribbean, it was to Africa that I always wanted to return.

In all whilst with the Foreign Service, I spent about 15 years in Africa working in Nigeria, Ethiopia, Uganda and Sierra Leone and visiting most other African countries for the OAU (Organisation for African Unity, now the African Union) meetings and as a member of the Foreign and Commonwealth Office's West African department. Since my retirement in 2002 I have continued to visit Africa, especially Sierra Leone 2/3 times a year. I can safely say that over 35 years of my life have been devoted to Africa in one way or another.

What has been the attraction? Certainly none of the countries in which I served could have been described as 'easy'. When I presented my credentials to President Kabbah in Sierra Leone in 1995 as the new British High Commissioner, I noted that I had served in Nigeria in the 1960s during the Biafran civil war, in Ethiopia in the 1970s during the revolution which removed Emperor Haile Selassie, in Uganda in the 1980s during two coups and constant insecurity, and so how nice it was to come at last to a stable African country. How ironic was that! Six weeks later we had the military coup in Freetown.

Nonetheless I have thoroughly enjoyed all my times in Africa. I found the work much more satisfying and rewarding. I felt that there was much more opportunity to make a difference for the better, albeit only small, to the lives of those in the various countries in which I was serving. How many of my brighter colleagues working all hours day and night in places like New York or Washington, Brussels, Paris or Bonn, could say that?

Moreover, working in Africa gave me a better understanding of the priorities of life, a better sense of what was important. On my returns to the UK for leave, etc, I would despair at what seemed to be focussing the attention of the people back in Britain, if looking at the front pages of the daily tabloids and listening to their conversation was anything to go by – some soap star having an affair, some footballer getting drunk, some comedian eating a hampster. Coming back from countries where thousands were dying of starvation, where hundreds were having their arms and legs hacked off, life in the UK sometimes seemed so petty and ephemeral.

And then there were the positive things in Africa, The beauty and majesty of the topography, the spectacular sight of the Nile being squeezed between two rocks 17 feet apart at the Murchison Falls in Uganda, the African sky at night where the air is so clear you feel you can touch the stars; the warmth and generosity of the people who though they have nothing will share what little they do have, who will never turn away some distant member of the extended family; the sacrifices made for a child's education; and the humour and vibrancy of Africans in the face of countless difficulties.

I have tried to capture some of all this in the telling of the anecdotes which follow.

Read and enjoy.

Peter Penfold
Abingdon
2021

The Most Contented Man in the World

THE MOST CONTENTED MAN IN THE WORLD

I met the most contented man in the world when I was working in Kaduna in Northern Nigeria at the end of the 1960s. His name was Musa and he was a Nigerian farmer living in a mud hut in the middle of nowhere. It was by mere chance that I met Musa.

After working for three years at the British Embassy in Bonn on my first overseas diplomatic posting, I was back in the Foreign Office when I received a phone call from the Personnel Department and was told to pack a suitcase and go off to Kaduna in a couple of weeks. Kaduna? I didn't know where Kaduna was. It was certainly not a place I would have asked to be posted to. But thank heaven that was how postings were arranged by the Foreign Office in those days – no post preference forms to be completed, no posting committees to be interviewed by, just pack and a bag and go. My assignment at the Deputy British High Commission in Kaduna was to be the start of a long and rewarding association with Africa.

So off I set in the footsteps of Burton and Speke, Clapperton and Mungo Park, to "discover" Africa. However, unlike these adventurous explorers, my "footsteps" would be motorised. As a "second poster" I was now in the fortunate position of buying my first brand new car, thanks to a car loan from the Foreign Office. I ordered a gleaming white Ford Cortina.

During my time in Germany I had become interested in car rallying. Many weekends were spent hurtling around the winding back roads of the Rhine valley with the Exiles Motoring Club in a little white MG midget sports car. I was the navigator. The driver, the owner of the car, happened to be one of the very attractive secretaries in the Embassy, which added to the attraction of the pastime.

I maintained my passion for rallying in Nigeria and found a few fellow enthusiasts. We decided to organise a rally and with my previous experience I offered to plan it. So one hot dry Sunday afternoon (nearly all days were hot and dry in the north of Nigeria) found me and my new girl friend at the time driving around plotting the rally course.

Quite frankly this was a bit ridiculous. In Germany when plotting a rally course, one would use the appropriate Landkarte (map), but in Nigeria there were no maps suitable for rallying. This was not that surprising because there were virtually no roads. In Kaduna itself, one of the biggest towns in the north, there were only two main roads. On one was situated the Hamdala Hotel and the offices of the High Commission and the British Council and on the other the Kingsway Stores – Kaduna's supermarket, though I use the term with reservation as often all you would find on the shelves would be packets of soap powder and tins of dried milk powder.

The two roads came together at a T junction, (not even a cross roads), but it was considered important enough to warrant the establishment of the first traffic lights in the whole of the north. There was great excitement when they were erected. People came from miles around by foot, bicycle and the occasional car or truck to gaze upon the flashing lights like the Blackpool illuminations. People would watch with awe and amazement as the lights changed from red, to red and amber, and to green. Once the lights had returned to red the spectators would realise that they had seen all the various colour combinations and they would move on, including the motorists oblivious of the instructions to stop on red and go on green. Perhaps not surprisingly this led to an early accident between a car and a truck. The car bounced off the truck and into one of the traffic lights, which bent over smashing the light bulbs in the process. After that the lights never worked again all of the two years that I spent in Kaduna.

The two roads were tarmaced, or to be more precise, were ribbons of potholes joined together with tarmac, but once you left the environs of the town they reverted to the traditional covering of laterite, red shale which threw up clouds of thick red dust which permeated everything as you drove along.

From Kaduna you could head in three directions – south to Ilorin and eventually the capital Lagos, northwest to Sokoto and northeast to Kano. I was driving along the southern road in my new Ford Cortina, its gleaming white paint now replaced with a russet hue from the laterite. I held a pencil and paper on my lap to plot the rally.

The essence of a car rally is not just the driving but also the navigation. The challenge is to follow a complicated set of navigational instructions often entailing turning off down back roads and country lanes. In Nigeria this was

The Most Contented Man in the World

not easy. Once you set off along one of the laterite "highways" you could keep going for dozens of miles before you came to another "road". So there I was devising the "herringbone" and "tulip" sections of my rally but without any roads to turn off on.

A few miles out of Kaduna I saw a narrow track leading off into the bush. It looked as if a car might just be able to get along it so we turned off.

The track was flat and dusty. I had not been able to afford the optional extra of air conditioning. When purchasing a car in those days everything seemed to be an "optional extra", even driving mirrors and windscreen wipers. As we drove along the hot dusty track we had the option of either winding the windows down and sitting in the inside of a Hoover dustbag or keeping the windows closed and roasting in a microwave oven. We alternated and consequently the beads of sweat mixed with the grime of the dust on our faces, necks and hands – this was fun?

Suddenly in front of us I could see a pool of water covering the track. I stopped and was immediately engulfed with dust all around us. As the dust settled I got out and walked along the track up to the water which stretched about ten feet in length and about a foot either side of the track. But how deep was it? Could I get through in my Cortina?

I picked up a long stick, walked round to one side of the pool of water and poked the stick in. It went down about six inches. That's not bad, I thought to myself, we can get through that. I went back to the car and assured my partner that we would be alright. I proceeded to drive slowly into the water. Barely had we touched the water when we lurched to one side. The car came to a halt with us leaning at a thirty degree angle. I had poked my stick six inches into one side of the muddy water and foolishly had assumed that the pool of water was uniformly six inches in depth. In fact, the track sloped at that point and the other side of the track was nearly two feet in depth. We were stuck.

Now usually it is a feature in Africa that you seem to be in the middle of nowhere with no sign of any habitation but when you stop, suddenly from out of nowhere you are surrounded by dozens of local people who appear as if by magic. But on this occasion no-one appeared.

We clambered gingerly out of the car into the muddy water fearful of the tales of the dreaded bilharzia which lurked in the water. We tried pushing the car but it would not budge. Our earlier amusement began to turn to apprehension. What to do? The AA did not reach Nigeria and this was still before the days of the mobile phone. We would have to go for help.

But this raised a problem in my mind. Did we both go for help leaving my lovely new car exposed to the dangers of Africa? Would we return to find an empty shell? Or should one of us go and the other remain behind, and if so which one? In those days in Nigeria, even with a civil war going on in other parts of the country, one always felt safe. The Nigerians, especially the Hausa in the north, were very friendly and hospitable. To my mind the greater risk was to leave the car to be discovered by some passing Nigerians who would assume that it had been abandoned and therefore they would be perfectly entitled to help themselves to the odd wing mirror and windscreen wiper, not to mention window or car-seat.

The decision made, I left my companion sitting on top of the bonnet whilst I trudged off further along the track. I knew there was little point going back. We were a good couple of miles from where we had turned off from the laterite and we had passed nothing up to that point. Surely the track led to somewhere and hopefully not too far further ahead.

I walked for about a mile when I came to a clutch of two or three mud huts – civilisation! Outside one of the huts, perched on a wooden chair, sat Musa.

I went up to him. He seemed a little bemused to see me. I greeted him in my basic Hausa which I had been trying to master since my arrival in Nigeria. Hausa is a very old and beautiful language. One takes one's time learning it and speaking it. There is not one simple word for "hello". A simple greeting is indeed a conversation. You go through a whole retinue of sayings when greeting another person. "How are you? How are your children? How are your wives? How are your neighbours? How is your farm? How are your crops? How is the rain that feeds your crops? How are the locusts which eat your crops?" I went through the elaborate greeting and introduced myself as "Peter" to which he told me he was "Musa".

An interesting feature of the ancient Hausa language is how it has assimilated modern terms into its vocabulary. For example, the name for a house or hut or any edifice is "gidan". When the first post offices were erected around the country they were used both for the delivery of letters and also to house the village telephone. People were fascinated with these buildings connected with the telephone wires, hence the name for a post office in Hausa became "gidan waya". (I was told that the name for a woman's brassiere in Hausa was "knickers-for-up"!)

In my limited Hausa I tried to explain my predicament to Musa. With a combination of words such as car and water and a visual demonstration of being stuck in the mud, I managed to get the message across. He was ready to come along but clearly decided that this was too much fun, and possibly and opportunity for pecuniary advancement, not to be shared by some of his family and fellow villagers so he despatched one of the small children who had appeared from inside the hut to find some other helpers.

It was while I sat with Musa waiting for the others to arrive that I contemplated that this was the most contented man I had ever met. In front of Musa's hut was a small stretch of land on which were growing some very fine looking crops – some cassava, grain, a few tomatoes, onions. Once a year Musa would plant his crops and once a year he would harvest them. For the rest of the year he would sit on his wooden chair and watch them grow. Inside the round hut was a bed and a few belongings, and in the middle of the earth floor was a fire on which one of his several wives or children cooked the food which he was growing outside. A goat was hanging around the back of the hut from which he got some fresh goat's milk.

There was no television to warn him about all the terrible things going on in the world. He did not even own a radio, he informed me, (was this a hint?), but the headman had one and he would keep people informed about what was going on such as which football team had won or who was now governing the country. He had no problems over plumbing, sanitation or electricity – there were none. He didn't need a light to read, he couldn't read. There were no school or medical bills to pay, there was no school or clinic in the village – the nearest were back in Kaduna, which he had visited about three times in his life.

And yet with all this deprivation, he was a contented man. He shouldn't have been. Didn't he realise that he needed to read and write? Didn't he realize that he needed to have health care, a road into the village, fertiliser to grow more crops, a telephone, life insurance, mosquito netting, etc. But this was the age before the NGOs had reached his village. They would come in the next decade and soon tell him that his life was miserable and that he needed all these other things to live a happy and productive life. For now all he could do was sit and watch his children play and his crops grow.

Musa and his friends came back down the track and we pushed my car out of the muddy pool. We pushed it back along the track we had come and managed to turn it around to head back to Kaduna. I gave Musa a few Nigerian shillings (the Naira had yet to be introduced) to share amongst his friends. I think that they were a little puzzled what they would use them for – possibly that radio? Of more use I gave him a spare shirt and pair of shorts which I had in the boot of the car and some sweets and biscuits to much delight of the children.

I refrained from suggesting that perhaps they should drain the pool of water and level it to allow more rally planners to visit his village. That would come later but for now Musa was content and why should I spoil it for the world's most contented man?

I learned a valuable lesson that day I met Musa which stood me in good stead for the rest of my career in Africa. Of course international aid agencies and NGOs (non-governmental organisations) can and have played a useful role in the development of African countries, especially in the areas of health, education and job creation. However, in my view, it is equally important to respect the culture and traditions of these countries. Recreating and copying what we have in our own home countries is not always necessarily the best thing to do. Sometimes we can also learn from Africa.

Chapter Two

TALES FROM KADUNA

I have always maintained that you can be much happier living in Africa than in "the west" by applying what I call "the Penfold Happiness rule". In Africa, when you flick the switch and the light comes on, it makes you happy; when you turn the tap and water comes out, it makes you smile; when you go to the garage and they have petrol, you clap your hands; when you go to the local store and they have more than soap powder and bars of soap on the shelves, you feel good. People living in Britain and other so called civilised countries do these things every day and derive no happiness from them.

It was my first posting to Nigeria that introduced me to this assortment of happinesses as I went about my day to day living in Africa, though others called them frustrations. Expatriates who have worked in Africa can give endless examples. I am particularly fond of this one from my time in Kaduna.

Kaduna in the north of Nigeria had originally been established as a colonial regional headquarters by Lugard at the turn of the century. By the end of the 1960s when I was posted to the Deputy British High Commission there, the number of expatriates had dwindled but the old colonial "Kaduna Club" was still running. Its days of colonial splendour had faded. Bulb-less chandeliers hung from the ceilings, the paint was peeling off the cracked walls and holes appeared in the termite eaten wooden floors on which sat an assortment of large broken arm-chairs. Once a week film shows would be put on. One of the outside walls had been painted white and we would sit outside under the stars on our deck chairs that we had brought along in the cool evening air. To the hum of an old 16mm projector we would watch old films that the British Council had managed to send out from the UK in years gone by and had never been returned. Abdu, the barman, doubled as the projectionist. It was fairly common for him to mix up the reels of film showing them in the wrong order. For example, if it was an Agatha Christie mystery, we would know at the start "who done it", but we had to wait to the end to find out what he had done!

The Kaduna Club was a favourite watering hole for some of the expatriates working in the area and occasionally I would stop by on the way home from work for a gin and tonic and a chat. One of the regulars was a Dutchman called "Kemp". I don't know what Kemp's real first name was. Everyone called him Kemp from his surname Kempenaar. Kemp was the manager of the local Ford Service Depot and he always had an amusing tale to tell from that day's exertions. This particular day Kemp was sitting in his usual place at the bar and was already into his third Star beer. Confident of getting him going by lining up another bottle, I asked him how his day had been. "Oh Peter, you'll never believe what happened today", and he related this tale.

A car had been brought into the workshop for repair. It had been in a crash and the whole of one side wing had been bashed in. Most of the dents had been hammered out but there remained a gaping hole still in the side. Kemp called his mechanics around him and explained that they would have to weld another piece of metal onto the wing. They looked a little puzzled. Kemp was standing next to the big enclosed water-tank in the yard and he took out a piece of chalk and drew a large rectangle onto the side of the tank; he explained that they needed to find a piece of metal the size that he had just drawn and weld it onto the car.

Kemp went back to his office. About an hour later he returned to see how they were getting on. He was horrified to find that they had cut out a piece of the water-tank, following very carefully the chalk lines he had drawn, and were about to weld it onto the car. He told them that before they did anything else they would have to repair the water tank by welding the piece of metal back into its place. He went back to his office.

A little while later he returned. He was delighted to see that the piece of metal was welded back onto the side of the water tank. But as he approached he could hear a knocking sound, and it was coming from inside the tank? In order to keep the piece of metal in place while it was welded back onto the tank, one of the mechanics had sat inside holding it. The said mechanic was now firmly trapped inside the sealed tank! Another hole had to be cut to get him out before he suffocated.

The African's ingenuity in fixing things such as cars knew no bounds. Indeed in most of the missions in which I worked in Africa we would have "a fixer", a member of staff specifically designated to fix any problem which arose. Our fixer in Kaduna was a giant of a man called Hassan. Hassan was a Hausa who went around wearing a huge cowboy hat. One time the wing mirrors on my car were stolen. I went to Hassan and asked if he could get replacements for me. Hassan said he would go down to the local market. Later that day he reappeared clutching two gleaming Ford Cortina wing mirrors which he duly fixed to my car. That evening I was at a cocktail party when a friend sauntered up to me and said somewhat disconsolately: "You'll never guess what happened to me this afternoon? Someone stole the wing mirrors off my new Ford Cortina". Commiserating with my friend, I wandered away without revealing to him that his wing mirrors were almost certainly now attached to my car outside. I was sure that his fixer would be able to find replacements.

Kemp's story revealed how careful one had to be in giving instructions to those with whom you were working. What seemed straightforward could often be misinterpreted, or, to be more precise, interpreted literally. There was the tragic tale of the couple who were going out to dinner and they told their babysitter: "There is some milk in the fridge. If the baby wakes, give it the milk and then put it back in the fridge". When they returned home they found the baby in the fridge.

Such stories may sound far fetched but to the African, especially those who had come in from the remote villages, what the expatriates did and said was a constant source of bewilderment and amusement. I remember listening to the news over the radio when the American astronaut, Neil Armstrong, first set foot on the moon. I wandered out into my garden and gazed up at the moon. Ibrahim my gardener was tending some plants. I called him over and pointing up at the moon, I said: "Ibrahim, you know that right now there is a man walking on the moon". Ibrahim looked at me and without a flicker of excitement merely replied "Yes, sir," and went back to his digging. He clearly thought that I'd had one too many gins and tonic – these crazy expatriates!

Chapter Three

A BRIDGE TOO FAR

You can never judge a book by its cover and you can never judge a country by its capital. It is so important to get out of the capital and explore, otherwise you can never really appreciate the country nor understand what is going on. This has been true of all the countries in which I have served.

Ethiopia was a marvelous country for exploring. It is a country so rich in history and culture. Ethiopians do not regard themselves as Africans, nor as Arabs, they are a race unto themselves, and with a history stretching back as far as the Queen of Sheba and beyond.

In 1975 I set off on a trip from the capital Addis Ababa. I would be visiting two of the provinces – Kaffa in the south-west and Wollega in the west. My traveling companion was Tadessa, one of the drivers at the Embassy.

In 1975 Ethiopia was going through its revolution. Emperor Haile Selassie was still alive but the soldiers were gradually eroding all his power and taking over. It was known as the "creeping coup". The country was effectively being run by a committee of middle ranking military officers – the Derg (the Amharic name for committee). Major Mengistu Haile-Mariam was one of its senior members but he had yet to shoot his way to the top.

The country continued to suffer from the various droughts and famines, for which it became synonymous. The economy was in bad shape. Traveling around the country was very difficult, not least because there was no petrol once you left the capital, hence it was necessary to carry all your fuel with you. With such a long journey planned, the normal 5 gallon jerry cans were not enough so before setting off, Tadessa and I put a 50 gallon drum of petrol in the back of the landrover.

Our first port of call was the town of Jimma, the capital of Kaffa Province. The province is noted for its coffee growing, indeed it is believed that the name coffee comes from the name of the province. We made the trip after a 13 hour drive having set off before dawn had broken over the capital. In Jimma we stayed at a reasonable guesthouse for a couple of days completing a series of visits and calls arranged by the provincial administration. It was a fairly rare sight for such officials in the far flung provinces to receive visiting diplomats from Addis and although I was a mere Second Secretary, I was given a very hospitable welcome. Tadessa and I were sorry to leave but we had to move onto Nekempt, the capital of Wollega Province for the next part of our programme. But this presented something of a problem.

The road system of Ethiopia was like the spokes of a bicycle wheel. All roads led to and from Addis Ababa but they did not connect up. This meant that we would have to drive all the way back to Addis to then drive along the western spoke to Nekempt. I did not fancy doing this. Nekempt was only about 120 miles north of Jimma, as the crow flies, whereas it was 160 miles back to Addis and then another 160 miles to Nekempt. I suggested to Tadessa that we find a track heading north and as long as we kept going northwards we would be bound to connect with the road heading west from Addis to Nekempt. Tadessa did not seem all that keen but I assured him that I had a compass and that we would be alright.

So off we set. We found a camel track heading north a little way out of Jimma. It was not very wide but the landrover was able to negotiate it. A small gully ran down the middle of the track caused by water erosion which our landrover straddled. However, the further we went along the track, the wider this gully became, so much so that we were no longer able to straddle it. It had also become somewhat deep with the consequence that we fell into it. I found myself on my side in the gulley with Tadessa on top of me. The petrol from the fuel drum was starting to ooze out filling the landrover with its pungent and inflammable fumes. To make matters worse, all this happened close to where the local farmers were burning their crops. It was a little unnerving. However, Tadessa kept his cool. He put the landrover into low gear ratio and 4 wheel drive and with some careful rocking to and fro he managed to drive the vehicle up the side of the ravine. We continued on our way, with the windows wound down to allow the pungent petrol fumes to escape.

The track continued to head northwards and we seemed to be making good time. I had just one concern. Looking at the map I could see that between us and the Addis/Nekempt road was a river – the Omo River, one of the major rivers of Ethiopia. I was gambling on the hope that the river would not be too deep and that we would be able to find a crossing point. If not, I thought, we can always float the landrover across!

By early afternoon we reached the Omo. I was concerned to see that in fact although it was the dry season, the river was fairly full and flowing fast. However, imagine my delight to see a splendid girder bridge across the river. The bridge was not marked on my old map. It had been built by the Italians during their occupation of Ethiopia in the Second World War. It was a fine bridge, a sturdy bridge, and one that reached all the way across the river. But there was just one problem. The river bank leading up on to the bridge had eroded away, and so the end of the bridge was three feet up in the air.

I told Tadessa that we would have to build a ramp up on to the bridge. There were plenty of the sweet smelling Eucalyptus trees around us and we had an axe in the back. We set about chopping down some trees and sloped them up from the ground onto the end of the bridge. It was hot work but after an hour or so we had built a fine looking ramp. While I remained on the bridge, Tadessa got back into the landrover and with me guiding him he carefully drove up the ramp and onto the bridge. We hugged one another in congratulations.

We drove along the bridge but pulled up sharply because there was the same problem on the other river bank. That too had eroded away, not quite as much as on our side, but we faced about a 2 foot drop.

I was tired from our previous exertions and did not welcome having to build another ramp. I suggested to Tadessa that we drove off the end. If we could get up enough speed, the momentum would carry us off the end and we would land on the other side. This was a good strong British landrover. The landing may be a bit sharp but the vehicle should take it. Tadessa looked at me apprehensively. I assured him we would be alright, although to keep the weight down in order to build up the speed, I would wait for him on the other side.

We backed the landrover along the narrow bridge right to the far end. I encouraged Tadessa to get the engine reving with the hand-brake on and then to release the brake and "fly". Tadessa reved up the engine and released the brake. I had expected the landrover to start like a Formula one racing car but in fact it seemed to move off very slowly. Gradually it picked up speed as it approached the end of the bridge. I could see Tadessa's face full of apprehension as he came to the end of the bridge but he kept going and then he was in the air. The landrover cleared the end of the bridge, almost. As it crashed to the ground, the back of the landrover caught the end of the bridge. It reared up like a horse kicking its hind legs and came down to earth again. I rushed across to check whether Tadessa was alright. He was badly shaken but otherwise OK. We went to inspect the back of the landrover. There was a big dent in the back door and the door handle had snapped off, but otherwise it looked OK. Fortunately the door could be opened so that we could have access to the drum of fuel. We tied the door closed and continued on our way.

About a half an hour further on we came to the main road. Tadessa was amazed to see it and his faith in my navigation was restored.

We drove into Nekempt and checked into its only guesthouse. We were hot tired, hungry and thirsty. Some lukewarm beer quenched our thirst and we ordered some food. Usually on my trips up country I would eat the national dish of injera and wat. Injera is made from a wheat grain called "tef". It looks and tastes like foam rubber. The wat is a kind of stew which is dumped in the middle of the injera. You break off chunks of the injera and dip it into the wat and then eat it. (In polite circles you actually feed one another).

I never found injera and wat particularly appetising but was happy to eat it. However, on this occasion the guest house insisted on cooking me a "European meal". This turned out to be a sort of stew with dumplings but within an hour of eating it my insides were erupting. I think that they must have left the meat hanging up outside for the last week in the hot sun. I went to my room and then spent the whole of the night clinging to the toilet seat, when I was not sitting on it!

When morning came I was still there. I felt awful. I told Tadesa that there was no way that I could carry out my programme of activities. I called on the Provincial Governor and explained that I was going to have to return to Addis Ababa immediately. Though disappointed he could see the state that I was in and waved me off outside his office.

We drove back with me groaning in the front seat along side Tadessa. He wanted to stop but I told him to keep going. All I could think of was to get home to my bed and die.

We finally reached Addis and I went straight to bed while my wife called for the Embassy doctor to come around. Dr Gordon confirmed that I had food poisoning and kept me in bed for a couple of days.

By the time I returned to work the interest about what had happened to the back of the landrover had subsided but I assured our transport officer that Tadessa was in no way to blame for the damage – the fault was entirely mine. The transport officer informed me that, immediately upon his return from our up country trip, Tadessa had put in a request to be taken off driving the landrover for journeys outside the capital and instead asked to be assigned to driving the Cortina saloon around the city - where there were no bridges to cross!

Chapter Four

BUMP-STARTING A FOKKER

An integral part of the African adventure is the thrill and excitement of flying around the continent. Whenever two or three experienced African hands are gathered together they become members of the 'whenwe tribe' – 'when we were in so and so, etc. Often the discussion will turn to 'journeys I have made by air in Africa'. My contribution is usually about the time we bump-started a Fokker aircraft.

It was in Ethiopia in 1975. I was flying back to the capital, Addis Ababa, from Gondar, the ancient capital of Abyssinia in the north of the country. I had spent the previous two months living with an English missionary as part of my Amharic language training and it was time to take up my post as Second Secretary at the Embassy in Addis.

Travelling around Ethiopia was not easy – (see the previous chapter). Ethiopian Airlines 'maintained' a fleet of old Fokker F27s, the Dutch built twin turboprop engine planes, providing a link between the capital and some of the remote provincial towns.

Half a dozen of us waited early in the morning on the grass strip which passed as the Gondar airport. We climbed on board the plane. There were no seats, just strips of canvas which ran down the two sides of the fuselage. We took our places and waited as the Ethiopian pilot tried to start the engines. He was obviously not having much success. Despite his constant attempts, the engines would not start. It seemed that the batteries were flat and Gondar airport did not boast one of those mobile charger trucks which one sees at sophisticated airports.

We watched the pilot climb out of his seat at the front and walk back down the plane to a cupboard at the back where he produced a large coil of thick rope. He jumped out of the plane and we could hear him shouting to various people who were hanging around – the airline official who had checked our tickets, a policeman who was leaning on his bicycle, a farmer who was tending his goats by the side of the runway.

Through the port-hole windows of the plane, we watched with fascination, and a degree of anxiety, as the pilot coiled one end of the rope around the propeller of the Fokker and then handed the other end to his group of volunteers. The pilot climbed back on board and resumed his seat at the front of the plane. On his signal the men outside started yanking at the rope whilst he fiddled with some of the switches in the cockpit. The propeller slowly turned round but spluttered to a halt. He got out of the plane and wrapped the rope around the propeller again. Resuming his seat, they tried again. The propeller turned a few more times but again came to a halt.

The exercise was repeated a third time. This time with a cough and a splutter, the engine came to life and the propeller started to spin faster and faster. With one engine turning, the pilot fired up the other engine and the plane started to shake uncontrollably as the plane slowly began to move.

The pilot taxied to the end of the runaway and turned the plane around ready for take-off. All the passengers eyed each other nervously. Was he really going to take off? Yes, he was. We rumbled down the runway and after what appeared an eternity, the plane slowly lifted off. We were in the air. We looked through the windows at the official waving to us below as he disappeared out of sight. The policeman could be seen cycling away from the airport, the farmer had gone back to tending his goats. None of them seemed perturbed which was a marked difference from the feelings of those of us encased in this rickety flying machine.

After less than an hour the plane started to descend. We peered through the windows but all we could see was a large lake below. There was no sign of any buildings. We landed by the side of the lake and over the roar of the engines the pilot announced that we had landed at Bahar Dar to pick up a couple more passengers.

Fearful of the engines cutting out, the pilot kept the engines turning at full rev with the brakes on, the chocks under the wheels and all of us being shaken to pieces jumping up and down on the canvas seat.

The extra passengers climbed on board and we took off again. An hour later the Fokker landed at Bole International Airport on the outskirts of Addis Ababa and disgorged a group of very pale looking passengers. I was much relieved to be back and for the remainder of my tour in Ethiopia I tried to avoid travelling around the country by plane!

The Fokker F27 was aptly named the Fokker Friendship and she became a close friend to many who served in Africa. Aircraft enthusiasts would marvel at the sight of these aircraft still flying around Africa while many of her relatives were sitting in museums back in Europe and the US. Notwithstanding my experience in Ethiopia, they were very reliable and tales of 'interesting air journeys' would often relate more to the efficiency and ingenuity of the African airline companies rather than the condition of the aircraft. The over-booking of seats or the non arrival of scheduled flights often dominated such tales.

Air Zaire, for example, used to operate a weekly flight from Kinshasa to Nairobi via Bujumbura. However, the landing fees at Bujumbura were so exorbitant that if there were fewer than four passengers to pick up, the Air Zaire flight would not bother to land. An announcement would come over the airport tannoy at Bujumbura that Air Zaire flight No so and so to Nairobi was now passing overhead at 37,000 feet. Would passengers please come back next week. Sometimes the flight would not appear at all. These would be the occasions when President Mobutu of Zaire had commandeered the plane to go shopping in Europe.

I experienced the problem of over-booking at first hand when I was flying from Entebbe Airport in Uganda to Nairobi. It was after the OAU heads of state meeting in Kampala in 1975. At the end of the conference there was a rush by delegates and other attendees to fly down to Nairobi to pick up their international destinations back home. A crowd of us assembled in the departure lounge of Entebbe airport. The East African Airways plane was waiting on the tarmac but it became pretty obvious that there were far many more of us waiting to board the plane, all with our boarding passes, than there were seats on the plane. Tempers were rising.

An agitated East African Airways official climbed on to one of the seats in the lounge and faced the by now angry mob. 'Ladies and Gentlemen, please calm down. There is a small problem over the allocation of seats. Some of you will not be able to board. But don't worry. We have laid on another plane.'

The atmosphere became relaxed. However, one elderly journalist who clearly had more experience of this type of predicament than the rest of us, asked the official what was the departure time of the extra flight. 'It took off an hour ago', was the reply!

Nigerian Airways were fabled for constantly over –booking their flights. On frequent occasions passengers would be left stranded at airports clutching their valid boarding passes. A colleague once told me of a novel way in which a Nigerian Airline official dealt with the problem. He assembled all the passengers at the foot of the aircraft and told them to all run round the aircraft before climbing up the stairs. Those who made it to a seat could stay, those who failed to find a seat had to leave the aircraft – a Nigerian version of 'musical chairs'.

Nigeria was a marvellous source of 'flying stories'. My favourite is of the Nigerian Air Force MIG jet fighter which had crashed. The pilot had bailed out and the Nigerian authorities had established a Board of Inquiry to try to discover why this relatively new gift from the Soviet Union had come down. The pilot was asked various questions. Eventually he was asked if he had enough fuel. 'Oh yes sir', he replied.

'How do you know if you had enough fuel?'

'I checked the gauge, sir.'

'What did the gauge say.'

'It was on "E" sir.' (Gasps of amazement from the Inquiry members.)

'What does "E" mean?'

'Enough sir.'

'So what does "F" mean?'

'Finished, sir, finished!'

Chapter Five

THE DONKEY AND THE CAMEL

When I told my eldest daughter that I was writing this collection of African Anecdotes, her immediate reaction was 'I hope you include the one about the donkey and the camel in Ethiopia'.

While I was serving in Ethiopia, Debbie was attending her boarding school, Huyton College, outside Liverpool. One of the downsides of diplomatic life was that it was usually necessary for your children to go to boarding schools once they reached secondary school age. However, the Foreign Office, in addition to contributing towards the tuition fees, did pay for the children to fly out to their parents during the holidays. This made holidays extra special and one tried to spend as much 'quality time' with your children as possible.

The British Embassy in Addis Ababa is situated on an 80 acre compound just on the outskirts of the city. When the Emperor Menelik II had established his capital in Addis Ababa, in order to encourage as many foreign countries to establish diplomatic missions, he gave each new legation a gasha (80 acres) of land on which to build their embassies. A number of Embassies were thus established, each one recreating a little of home on their gasha. For example, when one visited one's French colleague, it was like driving through a densely wooded French forest, the American compound was downtown Washington full of barriers and concrete buildings, while the Soviet compound at night resembled a Siberian detention camp. We modelled our compound on an English park, open spaces and benches, tennis courts, a club house and bungalow style offices and houses for the staff. Some of the original circular thatched roofed huts, called 'tukuls', were still on the compound. The noted explorer and writer, Wilfred Thesiger, had been born in one of them in 1910 when his father was serving in the legation.

To add to the attractiveness each house had a well cultivated flower garden in front as if in suburban England. Many of us also had our traditional vegetable patch in which we grew an array of onions, carrots, lettuce and cabbage. All manner of crops could grow in the well cultivated soil. A visiting botanist from the UK proudly told Derek Day, the Ambassador, that he had never seen such fine marijuana growing behind the Ambassador's residence! One of Derek Day's predecessors had to be flown back to the UK urgently suffering from food poisoning after his cook had mistakenly picked and cooked some poisonous toadstools for the Ambassador's breakfast believing them to be mushrooms.

Pets were somewhat restricted because of the high incidence of rabies in the country – no dogs or cats were allowed on the compound, but each family compensated with an array of other animals as pets. We had a pet rabbit; Ambassador Derek Day next door to us had a pet giant tortoise. There were also stables on the compound for a collection of horses. We kept two, scrumptiously called Mango and Strawberry, for when Debbie came out on holiday. A section of the compound was designated as a paddock for the horses to exercise. This also doubled as a short 9 hole golf course, which sometimes led to clashes of interest between the riders and the golfers. A team of Sudanese security guards patrolled and protected the compound day and night so it was safe for the children to roam around all over the compound and plenty for them to do.

Menelik selected the site of the new capital in 1889 on becoming Emperor but at the time the surrounding hills were fairly barren. He arranged for hundreds of the fast growing Eucalyptus saplings to be planted so that within a relatively short time the capital, which he named Addis Ababa, Amharic for 'New Flower', was surrounded by tall Eucalyptus forests. Of an evening as the temperature dropped the beautiful smell of eucalyptus wood burning permeated the cool night air.

Addis Ababa is just under 8,000 feet above sea level, therefore altitude sickness could be a problem. We were encouraged to drop down a few thousand feet every couple of months for our health. To facilitate this the Embassy acquired a small piece of land 200 kms south of the capital near the town of Shashamane alongside Lake Langano, on which we built two simple but comfortable cabins. Lake Langano was one of the few inland lakes in Ethiopia that was bilharzia free and thus safe in which to swim and canoe. Thus it became a popular place to visit during the school holidays.

The town of Shashamane was well known for something else. As Emperor, Haile Selassie was all powerful and ruled Ethiopia like a feudal monarch. However some people in Jamaica in the Caribbean went one step further and decided that he was divine, a black Messiah, that he represented the second coming of Jesus. Before he had assumed the title of Haile Selassie, his name had been Ras Teferi Makonnen and thus these followers became known as Rastafarians. Their numbers began to swell and expand to other countries. In the 1960s when Haile Selassie had visited Jamaica, some of them decided to go to Ethiopia to pay homage to their God. The Emperor didn't quite know what to do with them so he gave them a large piece of land at Shashamane on which they were allowed to live peacefully and grow their crops, including, of course, marijuana. They settled happily and their number increased to around 2,000. Sometimes we would visit them on our trips to Lake Langano. At one stage it was even suggested that the remains of Bob Marley, the famous Jamaican singer and Rastafarian, should be reburied at Shashamane but this caused consternation in Jamaica and nothing came of the idea. Sadly after Haile Selassie had been deposed, the military government under Mengistu confiscated most of the land and their numbers dwindled to around a couple of hundred.

To reach Shashamane, which was situated on the Trans African highway between Cairo and the Cape, one passed only a few villages and a couple of townships on the way. There was usually very little traffic so one could drive very fast on the very straight concrete road.

On one occasion a friend was making the journey to Shashamane. Driving at great speed he suddenly saw in front of him in the middle of the road a donkey, which had decided to cross from one side of the road to the other. My friend slammed on his brakes and tried to swerve around the donkey, but he hit it. Somewhat shaken, he got out of his car which had been damaged but not too badly to allow it to still be roadworthy. The same could not be said for the donkey. Unfortunately it was lying there dead. Immediately my friend was surrounded by a crowd of angry people only some of whom had witnessed the accident. They all started shouting, berating him and demanding compensation. It was impossible to determine to whom exactly the donkey belonged and as the crowd got bigger the situation turned nastier. My friend suggested that he should go back to the nearest township through which he had just passed and return with a policeman to help resolve the situation. One of the elders in the crowd was designated to accompany him.

So off they set in his damaged car back along the road to the township a few kilometres away. They tracked down a policeman in the town who jumped into my friend's vehicle and they all set off back to the scene of the accident. When they reached the spot, the crowd was still there; but no donkey. Where the dead donkey had been, there was now lying in the middle of the road - a dead camel!

However much my friend claimed it had been a donkey he had hit, he could not persuade the policeman. He was forced to pay the much bigger amount of compensation for the dead camel, plus of course expenses to the policeman, the local headman and countless others before he could continue on his way.

What had happened to the dead donkey? He had no idea. Where the dead camel had come from remained a mystery. Had it been freshly killed? Or was it kept somewhere permanently to cover such exigencies we would never know?

But when my daughter Debbie heard the story, she would never forget it.

Chapter Six

THE BBC WORLD SERVICE

For millions of people in Africa their day begins with listening to the BBC World Service. The BBC World Service signature tune is as familiar to Africans as their own national anthems. The BBC's African Service broadcasts two excellent programmes – "Network Africa" in the morning and then later in the day "Focus on Africa". These two programmes, combined with the BBC's World Service news broadcasts bring them up to date with everything of consequence and interest which is going on in Africa and the rest of the world. The voices of the various presenters are as well known as members of their own families. When we brought the Sierra Leone Blind School choir over to Britain for a tour in 2003, we invited Robin White, the former head of Focus on Africa, to meet the choir. The children were ecstatic. As far as they were concerned Robin White was the most important person in Britain, surpassed only marginally by The Queen.

The BBC's reputation for providing impartial and accurate reporting is second to none. It is a reputation thoroughly deserved. Africans wanting to know what is going on in their own country will far more believe what they hear on the BBC than what they hear on their own radio programmes. The following anecdote, which has passed into the BBC's folklore, illustrates this.

It occurred while I was serving in Ethiopia in the 1970s. At that time the Eritrean war was still raging, the longest running civil war in the world. From Addis Ababa it was very difficult to find out what was going on. The Derg, the military group which had taken over from Emperor Haile Selassie, were very wary of releasing any information about the fighting in the north. Diplomats were banned from flying to Asmara, the Eritrean capital, and attempts to go overland were thwart with difficulties. When the renowned British journalist, Jon Swain, attempted to visit Eritrea overland from Addis, he was kidnapped by the rebels and held hostage for several weeks (I had warned him!)

As the political reporting officer in the Embassy, I had to rely mainly upon the few brave Eritreans living in Addis to find out what was going on. But this was dangerous. All Eritreans were under constant scrutiny from the East German trained Ethiopian security services. Just being seen talking to a Western diplomat could lead to their arrest and imprisonment. I was very conscious of this and I went to great lengths to try to protect them. On occasions I would pick up one of my Eritrean contacts down some dark secluded street at night, hide him in the boot of my car, and drive back to the safety of the British Embassy compound. The compound was protected by a team of Sudanese guards but I could not even risk letting them see who was in my car.

I had one particular close contact, Ato Adugna. My predecessor, Iain Murray, had developed a close relationship with him and I had been fortunate to continue this. Adugna's information about what was going on in Eritrea had regularly proved to be accurate.

On one occasion Adugna told me about a terrible atrocity which had taken place in Eritrea. The Ethiopian army had gone into a village close to Asmara and slaughtered hundreds of Eritreans, including women and children. The next morning I duly reported this in a telegram to London.

By chance that day John Osman, the BBC representative based in Nairobi flew into Addis. John was one of the BBC's most experienced and respected correspondents, who had been around Africa for several years. He frequently visited Ethiopia and would regularly come and have lunch with me at home on arrival.

On this particular day, as we tucked into our sausages flown in from the NAAFI in Nairobi, I passed on the information which Adugna had given me the night before, without revealing the source but assuring John that he had proved to be reliable in the past. John immediately filed the story back to the BBC in London using my telephone in the house. That evening the story of the atrocity in Eritrea led the World Service news.

Just by chance I bumped into Adugna again the next day. Very excitedly he immediately said; "There you are, I told you what I said yesterday was true, it was on the BBC news last night!"

I refrained from revealing to Adugna that he was actually the source of the story. Though he knew that the atrocity had taken place, even for him the proof was the fact that the BBC had broadcast it.

Chapter Seven

IDI AMIN

I served in Uganda in the mid 1980s as the Deputy British High Commissioner. With two coups taking place within six months of each other, they were interesting and exciting times. But that was not the first time that I had been to this beautiful country, once described by Churchill as 'the pearl of Africa'.

A decade earlier, when I had been working in the embassy in Ethiopia, part of my duties as the Second Secretary in Chancery were to cover the OAU (Organisation for African Unity), whose headquarters were in Addis Ababa. This included attending various OAU meetings around the continent and in 1975 I was sent to Kampala to attend the OAU heads of state meeting. Every year all the African heads of state get together for a summit meeting. Given the erratic behaviour of African presidents of canceling appointments or of keeping people waiting for hours, (King Hassan of Morocco infamously kept Her Majesty The Queen waiting for two hours for a state banquet in Her Majesty's honour, for which HM was not amused), I always considered it one of the miracles of Africa that once a year the OAU managed to assemble all, or most, of the heads of state in the same place and at the same time, more or less.

This particular summit was viewed with more trepidation than most because it meant that, as the host President, Idi Amin was to assume the mantle of Chairman of the OAU. When Amin first came to power in 1971, it was with the blessing and support of the British Government, who regarded this British trained army officer as a better bet than the awkward Milton Obote. He soon came to be regarded as a buffoon with his outrageous rantings and ravings – for example demanding to be invited to Royal weddings and awarding himself the CBE – Conqueror of the British Empire. Initially this buffoonery masked the awful atrocities which he was perpetrating on the Ugandan people. Respected African leaders like Nyerere of Tanzania, Senghor of Senegal, Gowon of Nigeria and Sadat of Egypt regarded him as an embarrassment to Africa. Nevertheless they and most of their fellow African heads of state turned up in Kampala for the opening ceremony held at the newly built Nile Conference Centre.

I was seated in the press gallery. Britain had no standing in the OAU, not even observer status, so that in order for me to attend such meetings I had to masquerade as a journalist working for that famous newspaper "British Information Services". I peered down from the press gallery at the colourful assembly below.

Mobutu was there from Zaire with his leopard skin hat and cane with just a fraction of his delegation seated behind him. He had arrived with nearly a hundred in his entourage, including all of his cabinet and any others whom he considered might be tempted to overthrow him whilst he was out of the country. It seemed that at every annual OAU summit at least one head of state would learn that he no longer had a state to return to. Hence practically every President came with huge delegations which added enormously to the costs and logistics of holding the meetings. More than one country had gone bust as a result of playing host to such gatherings. The size of Mobutu's delegation was matched by Gadaffi's who had arrived from Libya in four jumbo jets.

Some of the largest delegations came from the smallest and poorest countries. I spotted Macias Nguema from Equatorial Guinea, the only Spanish speaking country in Africa. Later on I tried out my Spanish on him as he sat rather forelornely in the Conference Hall lounge. He lamented the fact that no other African leader spoke his language. One almost felt sorry for him until one realised that this was one of the most notorious despots on the continent.

Julius Nyerere from Tanzania was there in his trademark Maoist suit and Yakubu Gowon in his flowing West African robes. The Malawian delegation could easily be spotted all dressed in their heavy serge 3-piece pin stripe suits, an attire insisted upon by their president, Hastings Banda, who never came to such gatherings. Two other heads of state were conspicuous by their absence – the flamboyant Kenneth Kaunda of Zambia, who arrived a day late brandishing his trademark white handkerchief, and the distinguished Jomo Kenyatta from Kenya. Kenyatta, one of the giants of African history, never had any time for his neighbour Amin and he sent his seemingly somewhat nondescript vice-president, Daniel Arap Moi.

The assembly waited for the great showman. Finally, Field Marshall Alhaji Dr Idi Amin Dada CBE etc strode into the Conference Hall wearing a big cowboy hat and cowboy boots. To rapturous applause from most of the assembled delegates he was declared Chairman of the OAU.

After the opening ceremony all the invited guests, diplomatic corps and members of the press were asked to leave to allow the meeting to go into closed session. This meant theoretically that we would not know what was being discussed. However, the conference officials forgot one thing. As the meeting was essentially a mixed Anglophone/Francaphone/Lusophone gathering, simultaneous translations were provided throughout in English, French and Portuguese, (but not in Spanish for Nguema). Headphones were available to obtain the necessary translations. These headphones had also been provided at the opening ceremony for the guests and press corps, and as we filed out they forgot to take them off us. The range of the headphones extended beyond the conference hall and consequently we were able to follow the discussions back up in the press room in the conference centre. It took the organisers over a day to figure out how the press were able to report verbatim what was going on inside the closed meetings. The next day a bunch of menacing security officials bounced into the press room and confiscated the headphones, though one enterprising journalist managed to hide his and throughout the conference he would sit in the gents and listen in to the proceedings.

During the opening ceremony one strange event occurred which was to have a major impact on the conference. After Amin had been declared Chairman and while one of the other heads of state was making a speech to welcome his appointment, an aide came up to Amin seated on the dais and handed him a piece of paper. Amin read it and then got up and walked round to President Gowon seated at his desk. Gowon read the paper and then got up and walked out of the conference hall followed by most of his delegation. We watched this seated up in the press gallery and wondered what was going on.

Soon all was revealed when we tuned into the lunchtime BBC news. Lagos radio was reporting that there had been a military coup in Nigeria. Information was sketchy but the new government was declaring that Gowon had been overthrown whilst attending the OAU Conference in Kampala – the OAU curse had struck again.

The piece of paper which had been given to Amin was interesting. It was actually a telex message from the BBC in London to John Osman their East African correspondent based in Nairobi who had come up to Kampala to cover the conference. The message was alerting John to the news coming out of Lagos and asking him to get alongside Gowon. John never received the message. Ugandan security officials had intercepted the message and taken it straight to Amin. The first John was aware of the message was when he was arrested by Ugandan security and accused of being involved in the coup.

The events in Nigeria tended to overshadow the proceedings in Kampala which annoyed Amin. He saw the conference as a means of self publicity and aggrandizement and did not want other news stories diverting attention away from the conference. At vast expense he had launched a television service in the country just prior to the meeting to promote his image to the Ugandan people of a world leader surrounded by heads of state – the first African country south of the Sahara to have colour television, and at a time when the people could barely buy a bag of rice on the streets.

I was to have a little cameo in the events unfurling in Lagos. Information coming out of Nigeria was very sketchy. The telephones were not working and the borders were closed. Most of the Western journalists who covered Africa had come to the OAU conference. In Kampala the best source of information about what was going on in Nigeria was in fact the British High Commission. There was no US Embassy, it had been closed down. The Nigerian High Commission and hence President Gowon's delegation was dependent upon the scanty media reports whilst in the British High Commission we were receiving copies of the telegrams which our High Commission in Lagos was sending to the Foreign Office in London.

President Gowon was considered a friend of Britain and we were instructed by the Foreign Office to brief him on what was going on in Nigeria. Together with our Acting High Commissioner, Jim Hennessy, (Amin had expelled the High Commissioner, Dick Slater, a few months earlier), I found myself frequently going up to Gowon's hotel suite to brief him on events in his country based upon the reports our offices in Lagos, Kaduna and Ibadan were sending. Having served in Nigeria made me somewhat accepted by Gowon and his delegation and they discussed events openly in my presence. Early on it appeared that not all of the Nigerian army had supported the coup and initial reports suggested that some factions, especially in the centre and north of the country, were still supporting Gowon. I remember vividly one meeting when these events were being discussed. Some of the advisers around Gowon were trying to persuade him to fly back and fight. But Gowon responded to this by saying that he had already been involved in one civil war in his country, the terrible Biafra War, he was not prepared to subject his people to another, he would not return.

I have always regarded this decision by Gowon not to make his people suffer as very admirable and he remained high in my estimation of African leaders. From Kampala Gowon flew to Britain where he went into exile and actually became a student at Warwick University. He was to return to Nigeria several years later where he remained respected.

With all this going on in Nigeria, the conference in Kampala was not receiving much attention around the world. Amin began to lose interest. As Chairman he was getting through the agenda in double quick time. Thanks to our remaining set of headphones, we were able to follow what was going on inside the Hall. If someone like Nyerere stood up to argue the finer points of a resolution, Amin would bang his gravel and tell him to sit down, the resolution was clear, you either voted yes or no, there was no need to debate it. Even Gadaffi was silenced in this manner. As a result the conference actually completed its agenda ahead of time, unknown hitherto in the history of OAU meetings.

Consequently, prior to the formal closing ceremony, all the delegates were invited to Lake Victoria to attend a military operation which would demonstrate how the glorious forces of African liberation would defeat the oppressive forces of South African apartheid. Press corps and guests were also invited and we were to witness what has to be one of the most bizarre events in the OAU's history. I have devoted a separate chapter to it.

My final image of Amin was at the final press conference which took place at the Nile Hotel after the closing ceremony. It was a vintage performance by Amin. All the press corps were assembled outside the hotel on the lawn, awaiting the arrival of Amin from we assumed inside the hotel. As we waited patiently, still revelling in the morning's events out at Lake Victoria, we heard the roar of a sports car behind us. As we turned round we could see a Maserati speeding up the grassy slopes of the Nile Hotel gardens. Driving it was Amin, in one of his military uniforms bedecked in his medals. He skidded to a halt, knocking over one of the television cameras, jumped out and announced that he was ready to give his press conference.

Amin told the assembled press gathering that he aware that some of his fellow heads of state were concerned that he was now Chairman of the OAU but he had assured them that Africa's voice would never be better heard. As proof, he said, look at all of you. No other African President receives as much media attention as he does. Every word he utters is written down and reported around the world. He was, of course, right, but sadly what he had to say only confirmed in many people's minds outside Africa that African leaders were despots and/or buffoons.

I remember the reason the satirical magazine Private Eye gave for ending its series of humorous sketches supposedly written by Amin, was that however hard they tried to make them sound ridiculous and absurd, they could never compete with what Amin actually said! Africa was well rid of Amin but it took decades for his legacy to be erased and for the poor people of Uganda to recover.

Chapter Eight

HOW TO DEFEAT APARTHEID – AMIN STYLE

Under the chairmanship of Idi Amin the 1975 OAU heads of state meeting in Kampala had completed its business and all that remained was the closing ceremony scheduled for midday on the final day. We had assumed that the morning would be free but the previous day all the conference delegates and the diplomatic and press corps had received an invitation from His Excellency Alhaji Field Marshall Dr Idi Amin Dada, VC, DSO, MC, CBE, to join him on the shores of nearby Lake Victoria for a special event.

So off we all set along the Gaba road heading southwest out of Kampala in a fleet of cars and buses to Lake Victoria. Rows of chairs had been set up above the lakeshore, including massive armchairs in the front for the various heads of state, with Amin sitting in the middle on what looked like a throne. Directly about 250 yards across the water from us was Kiruba Island.

Everyone settled into their seats and the master of ceremonies for the occasion was introduced – General Mustafa Idrisi, Amin's notorious Chief of Defence Staff, whose reputation for barbarity was second only to Amin himself.

Dressed in battle fatigues, Idrissi announced in broken English that we were about to witness a military operation which would demonstrate how the glorious forces of African liberation could defeat the evil forces of South African apartheid. The island across from us, he explained, represented South Africa. On top of the hill in the middle of the island one could just make out a flag pole, from which the South African flag was fluttering in the breeze.

As Idrisi spoke we could hear the whizzing sound of two Mig Jet fighters from the Ugandan Air Force passing overhead. "That", said Idrisi, "was the aerial reconnaissance". It had lasted 20 seconds. Whether they had seen anything was unclear as we certainly could not see them. "Now begins the land bombardment", he added.

Four anti-aircraft guns had been set up along the lakeshore directly below us. They started firing their shells at the island. The noise was deafening. Through the smoke from the guns we could see that even though the island was a relatively short distance away and quite large, nearly all the shells were missing the island and splashing into the surrounding water. This caused a ripple of giggles from the audience.

Idrisi was alert to this. "You may have noticed", he shouted through the microphone over the noise of the guns, "that some of the shells are landing in the water." The giggles intensified. "That's because there is stiff naval resistance in the area", he explained.

After about 15 minutes the pounding of the guns mercifully stopped. (Heaven knows how much the shells must have cost?) Idrisi informed us "The landing of the glorious forces of African liberation will now commence". With that four helicopters swooped low over the assembled gathering and flew over to the island. The island was quite densely wooded. The four helicopters landed on the far side of the island out of sight from us on the shore. (Later we were to see only three helicopters take off again which prompted some spectators to suggest that one of the helicopters had crashed on landing.)

We started to hear the crackle of automatic gunfire from the island. Idrissi gave a running commentary of different places in South Africa which were falling to the glorious liberation forces. He got more and more excited as we all watched on in wonder and bemusement. "The enemy are retreating, the evil forces of South African apartheid are being defeated, soon we will see the end of the treacherous apartheid regime, the famous (I think he meant infamous) South African flag will be pulled down, and the glorious flag of African liberation will be raised in victory".

On top of the hill we saw the South African flag being lowered and we waited expectantly for the liberation flag to be raised; but nothing happened. Idrisi said again, "And now the glorious flag of African liberation will be raised". Still nothing. Idrisi tried one more time, and then gave up. Clearly the glorious forces of African liberation had forgotten to take with them their glorious flag.

Unfased, Idrisi announced that that was the end of the military operation. He concluded, "We have demonstrated to you all today that apartheid can be beaten by the military might of Africa". There was a ripple of polite applause from the audience, most of whom were clearly embarrassed.

Idrisi saluted and marched off. The Ugandan Chief of Protocol then came to the microphone and announced "Your Excellencies, ladies and gentlemen, I have great pleasure, on behalf of His Excellency Alhaji Field Marshall

Dr Idi Amin Dada, VC, DSO, MC, CBE, to invite you all to his wedding reception. There was a gasp from the audience. In the midst of all the gunfire and excitement, few had noticed that Amin had slipped away. He now reappeared, resplendent in a gleaming white military uniform, his huge chest totally covered in medals. And on his arm was a young attractive girl dressed in a full length white wedding dress.

This was Sara, who apparently sometime that morning had become Amin's fourth wife. She was Amin's latest concubine. She used to accompany Amin as his navigator when he took part in various car rallies. This led to her being given the nickname "Suicide Sara".

We gathered around the happy couple as they cut an enormous wedding cake, slices of which were then handed out to all the guests together with glasses of champagne and bottles of beer.

It was surreal. There, on a sunny morning by the shores of Lake Victoria, we had just witnessed the military defeat of South African apartheid and now we were celebrating the wedding of Idi Amin. It was a spectacle which I will never forget.

Chapter Nine

MEETING MUGABE

Robert Mugabe was one of the most famous and controversial leaders ever to emerge in Africa. For nearly four decades he dominated Zimbabwean politics and oversaw the economic demise of this once rich and prosperous country. He had become Prime Minister in 1980 following the Lancaster House Agreement which ended Ian Smith's UDI of Rhodesia. I had the pleasure of meeting him a couple of years previously.

In 1977 the OAU heads of state meeting took place in Gabon, the former French colony in West Africa. Thanks to vast oil deposits, and watched closely by the French Government, the Gabonese economy was strong and stable. Walking around Libreville, the capital, one could easily imagine that you were in an affluent French city. People drove around in their Peugeot taxis while others sat outside the cafes with their croissants and coffee. At the time Gabon boasted the highest consumption of champagne per capita of any country in the world, even higher than France. Indeed I remember Christopher MacRae, our non-resident Ambassador, based in Lagos, arguing with the Foreign Office inspectors that his allowance for entertainment in Gabon should allow for champagne being served at every meal. The inspectors would have none of it!

So off I set from Addis Ababa to report on the conference. Flying across Africa from east to west or west to east was always very difficult because there were so few airlines flying such routes. Usually the easiest way to fly across the continent was to fly up to a European airport such as London, Paris or Amsterdam and back down again; and in fact this is what I did. I caught a flight from Nairobi to Paris and then flew on one of the daily Air France flights to Libreville.

I arrived at Libreville airport along with several others who were attending the OAU conference and went up to the special desk which had been set up at the airport to process the conference arrivals. Britain was not a member of the OAU, nor had observer status with the organisation. Therefore we would arrange through the OAU Secretariat in Addis for me to be accredited as a member of the press corps, representing "British Information Services". I showed my diplomatic passport to the Gabonese official at the desk. He looked down the list of delegates but could not find my name. I suggested that he look down the list of the press corps. Sure enough, there was my name but he could not understand why I was on that list when I had a diplomatic passport. I explained that I worked at the British Embassy in Addis Ababa. Then why was I on the press list, he repeated. I tried to explain but this was too complicated for him and I was asked to wait while he processed all the passengers for the conference. A supervisor was summoned. I went through all the explanations again but to no avail. I watched as I saw all the others who had arrived for the conference, both delegates and press, being whisked off on the conference buses. The supervisor said that I could not enter Gabon, I would have to leave on the next flight!

This was too much. I remonstrated with him and finally I was taken to a tiny wooden building around the back of the airport terminal. There sitting at a small tidy desk was a Frenchman. He studied my passport as I once again went through my explanation. The Frenchman pondered upon my predicament and finally said OK I could enter the country.

I found the experience extraordinary. Here I was in this "independent" African country which had gained its independence from France in 1960 but yet it was still a Frenchman who had the final say over whether I could enter the country. It was symptomatic of the way most of the former French territories were run in those days. For many of them the number of French nationals living and working had actually increased after independence.

In contrast to the British, the French decolonisation process in Africa had been somewhat cynical. Britain's attitude under Macmillan's "winds of change" policy and in the face of agitation from African leaders like Nkrumah in Ghana, had been in essence "we don't think you're ready for independence but if you really want it (and for some like Sierra Leone even if you don't) OK off you go; here's a little bit of money, you must now stand on your own two feet, good luck!" The French attitude under De Gaulle was "so you want independence, OK, you can have your president, a new flag, a new national anthem, but we will continue to control your economy from Paris and we will put Frenchmen in all your ministries to help run the country!"

As a result the former French territories tended to be more stable and more advanced economically. There is an apocryphal story about Nkrumah in Ghana and Houphet-Boigny in the Ivory Coast. Nkrumah's rallying call was "political freedom for the masses" while Houphet-Boigny advocated "economic development before political freedom". They took their respective countries down these different paths and agreed to compare results ten years later to see who was right. Nkrumah, of course, did not last ten years. He was toppled in a coup. Houphet-Boigny stayed in power over 30 years and, with the close support of France, saw the Ivorian economy become one of the strongest in Africa. It is interesting to compare these different approaches to decolonisation. One aspect of preparing their territories for independence which I believe the French did better than the British was to train their future political leaders. Houphet-Boigny had been a minister in the French cabinet in Paris. To the British, it was unthinkable that someone like Nkrumah should be a British cabinet minister.

The only African leader to reject De Gaulle's terms for independence was Sekou Toure in Guinea. He maintained that he would rather have "freedom in poverty than independence in chains". De Gaulle was so incensed, he pulled every Frenchman out of Guinea taking with them, reputedly even the electricity wires and water pipes. The Guinean economy was ruined and still suffers to this day.

Having got my clearance to enter Gabon from the Frenchman, I finally made my way to the hotel where I was staying. I met up with my fellow diplomatic colleagues who also attended the OAU conferences. There were normally four of us - Henri Jacolin and Lou Janowski from the French and US embassies in Addis and David Buckingham from the Australian High Commission in Nairobi. They had flown in the previous day. They had not experienced the difficulties I had faced at the airport because they had been met by representatives from the French and US embassies in Libreville. Unfortunately Britain did not have a resident embassy. For the purposes of reporting on the conference, arrangements had been made for me to use the communication facilities at the US Embassy.

Before leaving Addis I had received instructions from David Owen, our Foreign Secretary at the time, to introduce myself to the three Zimbabwean nationalist leaders – Bishop Abel Muzorewa of the ANC, Joshua Nkomo of PF - ZAPU and Robert Mugabe of PF - ZANU.

Rhodesian affairs had continued to dominate the British Government's involvement in Africa ever since Ian Smith's universal declaration of independence in 1965 and in recent years it had also dominated the activities of the OAU, led by the so-called Frontline States – Angola, Botswana, Mozambique, Tanzania and Zambia. There had been several attempts to resolve the impasse caused by UDI and move the country to true independence. The British Government were about to table yet another set of settlement proposals under which Smith was to surrender power to a six month transitional government under a British administrator leading to democratic elections. From the British Government's point of view, it was very important to maintain a dialogue with the three potential future leaders of Zimbabwe, hence David Owen's instruction to me. I duly made arrangements to see the three men.

I first went to see Bishop Muzorewa. I went up to his hotel suite and knocked on the door. The Bishop opened it and invited me in. He was alone and he invited me to have tea. It was very pleasant. He waxed lyrically of his fondness for the British and after a very pleasant hour or so I came away thinking what a lovely man, how nice if he becomes President.

The next day I went to see Joshua Nkomo in his hotel suite. An aide opened the door and I was ushered into the brightly lit room to be greeted by Nkomo in front of the television cameras, which Nkomo had arranged to be present. This was the showman at work. He played to the television, attacking the Smith regime and calling for the support of his friends in Britain. The show lasted half an hour and Nkomo showed me out sending warm greetings to David Owen. I came away thinking, mm, not as nice as the Bishop, but we could probably do business with him.

Later that day I went to see Robert Mugabe. I knocked on his hotel door. An aide came to the door and I introduced myself. I was left waiting at the door while the aide went back inside. After a few minutes Mugabe came to the door. I explained to him that my Foreign Secretary, Dr Owen, had asked me to let him know that I was present in Libreville in case he had any messages he wished to send to the British Government. Mugabe looked at me coldly and said "I have my own ways of sending messages to your government", and he slammed the door in my face. I went away thinking what a nasty man, I hope he does not end up in charge!

These, of course, were just snap-shot impressions of three very different African politicians but in some respect I think my views coincided with the way the British government was treating them at the time. Yes it would have been nice to see the Bishop emerge as the leader of Zimbabwe, and if not him then Nkomo, but not Mugabe. But this was just wishful thinking on our part. Any close follower of Rhodesian/Zimbabwean politics knew that it was practically certain that Mugabe would emerge from democratic elections as the leader. If we had been more prepared to accept this and therefore tried a little harder to get along side him, perhaps we might have avoided some of the problems that were to happen later on. I wonder?

Chapter Ten

FOR QUEEN AND COUNTRY

When serving overseas a diplomat can be called upon to perform many duties for Queen and Country, some more unusual than others. One of the more memorable duties during my time in Uganda was to serve as a judge at the Namasagali School annual beauty pageant.

Namasagali College is located in a remote spot on the banks of the Nile between Lakes Victoria and Kyoga about 50 miles north of Jinja. This private school was established in 1965 as Kamuli College, the nearest town, as a joint venture of the Busoga Kingdom and the Mill Hill Fathers of the Roman Catholic Church. The first two headteachers were Mill Hill Fathers, Father Navel until 1966 and then until 2000, Father Damien Grimes.

Namasagali enjoyed a colourful reputation. Reputedly Humphrey Bogart and Katherine Hepburn had stayed there for a few days when making the famous movie, 'The African Queen'. The noted journalist and television presenter, Jon Snow, had taught there in the late 1960s when serving with VSO (Voluntary Service Overseas). In his book 'Shooting History' he described Namasagali as having 'a whiff of the colonies and a dash of the Spice Girls' where 'the skirts were high and so was the level of discipline'.

Among Father Grimes' passions were boxing and dancing. It was through boxing that he came into contact with Idi Amin and as a result, in the midst of the turmoil all around caused by the evil tyrant's antics, the school remained remarkably virtually untouched. His passion for dancing manifested itself in the staging of the annual dance and beauty contests at the school.

Father Grimes made early contact soon after I had arrived in Kampala to take up my post as the Deputy British High Commissioner and invited me to be a judge at the forthcoming annual school beauty pageant. I had no idea what I was letting myself in for but always eager to get away from the capital and explore other parts of the country, I set off late afternoon and made the four hour journey to the school.

On arrival I was greeted warmly by Father Grimes in his clerical robes and offered some refreshment while he attended to some last minute preparations. I met my fellow judges, mostly former students of the school, who were now senior civil servants or teachers. The pageant was due to start at 7pm but it was way past 9pm before I and my fellow judges were invited to take our seats alongside the catwalk which had been erected jutting out from the stage in the large school hall. Modern pop music blared out from the huge speakers.

The pageant was obviously based upon the format of the Miss World competitions as initially a succession of young girls and boys paraded in 'local dress', a collection of colourful costumes made from local cloth. Next came the evening dress and then finally the swimwear. Clearly there were more contestants than costumes as several times the same costume appeared but adorned by a different face and figure.

Judging was by no means easy. I detected from some of my fellow judges a certain bias depending upon from which 'house' the contestant came. Also, as with most African schools, the age range was very wide, even within the same class, anything from twelve to twenty years of age.

It went on and on into the night so that by the time we had selected our various winners in the different categories, it was gone 4 am. The presentation of the crowns and trophies took another hour so as we finally pulled away from the school to head back to Kampala the dawn was rising. It had been memorable and I was exhausted. What one does for Queen and Country! Obviously Father Grimes had been pleased with my performance as I was invited back in successive years; or was it that he could not find anyone else to undertake this herculean task?

One would have thought that I had learned my lesson about judging such contests. One starts off as everyone's friend and then as soon as the results are announced only the winner is your friend and the other contestants and more particularly their families view you with disdain and suspicion.

So it was something of a surprise that back in Kampala I accepted an invitation to judge the National Disco Dance competition. I had been asked because it was known that I used to frequent the local disco Clouds most Fridays (see the following chapter on A Very African Coup). The competition took place at one of the hotels in town. It was very noisy but great fun. I was the sole judge and I had little problem in choosing one young man as the winner. He went by the name of Sandy Mobile and it was amazing how he contorted his body to the throbbing disco music. His prize was a trip to the UK where he would represent Uganda in the World Disco Dance context. (I didn't know there was such a competition!) I realised why the organisers had asked me to be the judge. They had to ensure that their winner would be given a visa to get to the UK for the contest.

So we issued the visa to Sandy Mobile and off he went. I thought nothing more about him until a few weeks later when the organisers rang me to announce that Sandy had won the contest in London. Sandy Mobile from Uganda was the World Disco Dance Champion. Apparently he had caused quite a stir. Not only was his performance outstanding but people in UK were pleasantly surprised to learn that there were any discos in 'war-torn' Uganda, let alone that people felt safe going to them. Sandy presented a more positive image of Uganda than the one which people in the West had been used to. He was a real Ambassador for his country and a role model for the youth. When he returned I threw a party for him at my home at which he demonstrated the skills that made him a World Champion.

Having heard of my involvement with Sandy Mobile and his trip to the UK, I was approached by one of Uganda's leading musicians and entertainers, Jimmy Katumba. With his group, the Ebonies, Jimmy was in effect the Cliff Richard of Uganda, giving many concerts in Uganda and elsewhere in East Africa, where, among his repertoire, he specialised in singing Jim Reeves songs. He asked if I could organise a UK tour for him. I had to politely decline pointing out that I already had a full-time job but we remained close friends. I did suggest to him however, that if he did go to the UK he should adapt his repertoire to include more African songs. If people in the UK wanted to hear Jim Reeves songs, they would listen to Jim Reeves.

Jimmy had started life as a teacher. He started using his songs to get public messages across to the Ugandan people. This was particularly effective with the message about AIDs which was just starting to rear its head in East Africa. Initially the disease was known as 'Slims'. Sadly Jimmy, like countless others, was finally to succumb to the dreaded illness after I had left Uganda.

As a parting gift to the people of Uganda at the end of my tour I wrote a song, 'Uganda My African Home'. Jimmy Katumba and the Ebonies recorded it and it remained a popular song in Uganda. During my final week they organised a farewell concert for me – slightly different from the usual diplomatic farewells.

> 'When I think of the Nile
> It raises a smile
> And mem'ries come flooding back to me
> Of warm starry nights

Crested cranes in flight
Uganda is where I long to be.

Chorus
From the hills of Karamoja
To the waters of Kyoga
From Kigezi to Kidepo I have roamed
Seen the mists of Kabale
Got drunk on Waragi
Uganda my African home.

I have been to Soroti
And eaten matoke
Climbed the Rwenzori mountains high
I have sung with the Acholi
And danced with Banyankole
And always was sad to say goodbye.

I have seen a crocodile
By the banks of the Nile
Whilst camping at the Murchison Falls
I have been to Semliki
And there I met a pygmy
Who tried to sell me his wooden balls.

Chapter Eleven

A VERY AFRICAN COUP

"Peter Penfold, hero of the Kampala crisis, also has a fun loving side to his nature. Many nights he can be found at the infamous Cloud Nine nightclub in Kampala where the Ugandan ladies of the night hang out."

Extract from Grovel's piece in Private Eye, August 1985.

The telephone rang in my house on Kololo Hill at one o'clock in the morning. It was Joyce Heckman, President Obote's British born Secretary.

"Peter, the President has just telephoned me to say that the rebels have taken the Karuma Falls Bridge and are on their way. He is leaving and he advises me to get out".

This was worrying news. The Northern Acholi elements in the army had been grumbling at the way Obote was treating them, particularly over some recent promotions. If they had taken the Karuma bridge 140 miles to the north, there were only the loyal Obote troops at the Bombo barracks just outside Kampala to stop them from reaching the capital, and if Obote was already fleeing, their resistance would not last long.

Our High Commissioner, Colin Maclean, was back in the UK on leave and therefore I was Acting High Commissioner. My first concern was for Joyce and her husband. Joyce had worked for Obote since the time Uganda had become independent in 1962. Though now of mature years, she was still very attractive. She was one of a remarkable handful of British ladies who had worked for African Presidents such as Nyerere in Tanzania and Kenyatta in Kenya as they took their countries down the path of independence. Although British, she was totally loyal to Obote. Nonetheless in the short time I had been in Uganda we had developed a close friendship and I was concerned for her safety. Once the rebel soldiers hit Kampala, no-one who had been close to Obote would be safe. Although it was curfew, I had to get Joyce and her husband away from their apartment which was right in the middle of the city. I contacted our RMP team (the team of 5 Royal Military Police who were attached to the High Commission to provide security for the High Commissioner and staff) via our radio communications net and told them that we were going into town to collect Joyce and hubby.

While I was waiting for the team to get to my house, I telephoned my colleagues the American Ambassador, the French Ambassador and the UN representative to alert them to the worrying news. Next to the British community, these three were responsible for the largest numbers of expatriates resident in Uganda. I suggested to them that they meet at my house as soon as dawn broke. They did not have bodyguard teams and did not feel it would be safe to travel during the curfew hours.

I set off around 2 am into town with four members of the team. The streets were deserted and it was very quiet. We bypassed the military road blocks around the town and did not meet any mobile patrols. Trying to beat the midnight curfew was a regular game for some residents of Kampala which sometimes led to tragic results but by this time of the night most of those mounting the roadblocks or mobile patrols were asleep. We picked Joyce and her husband up and drove back to my house. Joyce was not one to panic but she was clearly worried what would happen.

By the time we had discussed events over a cup of tea and I had packed them off to bed, the dawn was beginning to break and I prepared for my meeting with my diplomatic colleagues. Whilst waiting for them I contacted all the members of staff via the radio network and told them to pack a bag and be prepared to move at short notice.

My diplomatic colleagues arrived and I briefed them in more detail about events. I told them that I would be moving all my staff and their families to the High Commissioner's residence and would be alerting the British community to stay in their houses. My colleagues were concerned but were more inclined to await further developments before taking any action. They left.

I telephoned the Duty Officer in the Foreign Office, known by the quaint term "Resident Clerk", (I was later to become one), and reported on developments. I then instructed all the members of staff to make their way to the High Commissioner's residence, taking with them as much food as they could. By now it was light and people were moving about the streets. They were clearly unaware of the events in the north and there was no sign of worry or panic. The sight of British High Commission vehicles driving around town, several of them with deep freezes jutting out of their boots, made for an incongruous sight.

We assembled at the Residence. There were about twenty five of us all told, including wives and children and British Council staff. I briefed everyone on the latest situation. I had chosen to go to the Residence because it was the biggest of our properties and was more secure than our other homes. I assigned various duties to everyone. The next most senior officer and my right hand man was Noel Guina, our First Secretary Commercial from Northern Ireland. I asked Noel to coordinate our contacts with the British community which numbered over 600 in Kampala alone. Using the telephone and our British community radio network, he contacted members of our community and told them that we were expecting trouble that day and that they should stay indoors.

By now it was mid morning and we were beginning to get reports of rocket and mortar fire being heard on the northern outskirts of the town. Not surprisingly this led to panic on the streets of Kampala as people fled to their homes. Soon the shooting could be heard from the centre of town and from around the golf course. The noise grew louder. Some members of the British community appeared at the gates of the residence and we took them in. They were followed by some Ugandans who sadly I had to turn away. I could not risk soldiers, government or rebel, claiming that we were harbouring suspected enemies as an excuse to attack our residence.

For nearly three hours the fighting went on and then there was a lull. From the reports we were receiving from various contacts in the British, Ugandan and diplomatic communities it was clear that the northern soldiers had the upper hand and were driving the Obote troops out of Kampala. I decided to go into the office in the centre of town to see for myself and to send a telegram reporting what had happened. I had been able to keep the Resident Clerk informed by telephone but this means of communication was not secure and also I needed the one telephone at the residence to keep in contact with people in Kampala.

I set off with my communications officer and two members of the RMP team to the office which was situated about half a mile away. There were many people on the streets. They were cheering and waving at truck loads of troops who were driving around brandishing their guns. We reached the office without incident. On the steps was James, one of our local security guards. This was the guard who famously, when the Tanzanian troops entered Kampala in 1979 to drive out Amin and his henchman, all alone stopped them from looting the building by saying to them "This is the British High Commission. You are not allowed to enter." And they went away.

I had already drafted my confidential reporting telegram alerting both London and all neighbouring African posts of the fighting and I was waiting in my office for Dave, the communications officer, to send it winging on its way when suddenly the shooting broke out again. I dived for cover as bullets came crashing through the windows along the corridor of the offices. I waited for the shooting to subside and shouted to Dave to hurry up and finish so that we could escape. I did not want to be trapped in the office with everyone else up at the residence.

During the break in the shooting we ran out of the offices, dived into the waiting Range Rover and drove back to the residence, this time a little more speedily than before. We could hear shooting all around us but we reached the residence without any incident.

By the time we had got back to the residence the numbers inside had swelled to around forty including some members of the community who had got caught up in the shooting while doing their Saturday shopping and others who had decided that the High Commissioner's residence would be safer than their homes. Our swelled ranks had also included three members of our military training team based in Jinja, fifty miles east of Kampala. I had alerted the team leader, Col John Lowles, of what was going on and he had immediately sent his young Para Captain, David Limb and two others to Kampala to help out. I was extremely glad to see them.

The shooting continued, some of it perilously close to the residence. By now it was becoming clear that it was not resistance from the fleeing Obote troops but the Northern soldiers, fortified by copious amounts of alcohol, were on a looting and pillaging spree. Shops and stores in town, especially those belonging to foreigners such as Asians, many of whom were British passport holders, came under attack. One British Asian, a Mr Patel, was killed.

As dark descended the mayhem continued and became more frightening. Inside the residence our numbers were now up to around fifty. There was no indication how long this would go on for and I realised that we would need to establish some degree of domestic order to cope with these numbers. Our Vice Consul was Maurice Brookes. Maurice was the longest serving of our UK based staff and well liked in the community, not least for the parties he would throw at his house for, as well as his joviality, Maurice was a cordon bleu chef. I asked Maurice to take charge of all the domestic arrangements making sure that we had food and bedding. Maurice was a little upset to be taken away from his consular duties but I pointed out that if we did not have order within the residence we would not be able to cope with all the other demands of monitoring events, keeping in touch with the community and keeping London informed.

Everyone was ordered to stay inside. Only our military team of the RMPs and the David Limb's group patrolled the large gardens surrounding the residence. I kept in touch with them from the High Commissioner's study through the walkie-talkies. At one point the shooting came very close. We could hear the bullets whistling around the outside of the building. I heard over the RMP radio Graham ask Vic "Can you see anyone?" Back came the reply "Not at the moment. I'm kissing the grass."

Inside the residence Joyce said "That gunfire, you can almost smell it", to which Dougie, our young ebullient Second Secretary replied "Smell it? I'm sitting in it!"

We continued to monitor the local radio station, which initially had gone off the air but was now back playing Ugandan music. From time to time the music would be interrupted by announcements from obviously drunken soldiers proclaiming that there was nothing to worry about, everything was (hic) under control. This would be accompanied by the sound of gunfire, sometimes coming from within the studio itself.

In the midst of the chaos outside Maurice produced a delicious meal of sausages and mash from the well stocked kitchen which was wolfed down by us all. Each time the shooting came closer people would dive to the floor. We tried to bed down for the night. Blankets and pillows were produced and people laid them out in different corners of the various rooms in the residence. We kept only a few lights on, not wanting to attract the attention of the marauding soldiers outside.

Throughout the night the shooting continued accompanied at times by screams of people being attacked by the drunken soldiers. I stayed in the study talking to Noel. Neither of us could sleep. It was far easier to receive phone calls than send them and I asked the Resident Clerk in London to call us every two hours to check that we were OK. It was somewhat comforting to feel that there was at least one person outside who was in touch with us.

Dawn broke. We were all still alive. I called everyone around and suggested that we say a prayer to thank God for bringing us safely through the night and for our loved ones away from us who must be worrying about us. Maurice then produced a hearty breakfast of eggs and bacon.

The phone now rang incessantly, mainly from friends and relations in Britain who were catching up with the news back home, and also the media. We were three hours ahead of Greenwich Mean Time. The BBC news rang through to say that they would like to conduct a live interview with me. They carried out a sound check and asked me to stand by for the interviewer. While I was waiting the gunfire opened up again outside. This time the bullets were strafing the building. I dived under the desk alongside the High Commissioner's dog who had taken refuge there. I was still clutching the phone. A very English voice said "We are now going to talk to our Acting High Commissioner in the besieged Ugandan capital. Mr Penfold how are you?" "As well as can be expected", I replied. "I'm sorry, Mr Penfold, we don't seem to be hearing you very well". "That may be because I am sitting under the desk." "Why are you doing that?" asked the voice from England. "Because there are bullets flying all around us," I shouted back. It seemed to me to be a very obvious answer given the situation we were in but apparently it made quite an impact upon the listeners in Britain as they tucked into their Sunday breakfasts!

Further announcements were made over the local radio, none of which offered us any comfort that the soldiers were coming under any degree of control. The shooting outside had generally subsided. The soldiers were either exhausted or had run out of ammunition. A false air of normality hung over the city. One of the British Asians, Mr Singh, who had taken refuge with us, asked me if I could fill up the residence swimming pool so that his family could take a dip!

I decided that I needed to go into town to try and find out who precisely was now running the country.

I contacted the American Ambassador and told him of my intention and asked whether he wanted to join me. He had taken refuge with all his male staff members in his Embassy which was right in the middle of town behind our High Commission offices. This had been a mistake. Not only was he in the thick of it but he had left all his staff's dependents scattered all around the city in their homes at the mercy of the marauding soldiers. I had continued to keep in touch with him over the radio. Clearly the situation in his offices was grim. They had neither slept nor eaten all night. The ambassador told me that he would join me but only if he could accompany me in my armoured Range Rover, the only one in the country. I agreed to pick him up.

I went to see Maurice in the kitchen and enquired what we would be having for lunch. Maurice looked at me quizzically and said in a matter of fact voice "Sunday roast, of course – roast lamb, roast potatoes and all the trimmings!" I asked whether he could prepare a little extra for me to take to the American ambassador and his staff.

We set off in a convoy of three vehicles, myself and two RMPs in the front in the armoured Range Rover with the Union Jack flying, the back-up RMP car behind us and David Limb and his team bringing up the rear. There were no other vehicles on the roads and the streets were practically deserted with just the odd person scurrying along. It was nothing like the usual bustling scene of a Sunday lunchtime. We saw some dead bodies lying by the side of the road and the full horror of what had happened through the night was sinking in. A number of cars had been abandoned, their occupants presumably dragged out of their cars. Groups of disheveled soldiers were wandering around clearly the worst for wear after their night of looting and debauchery. They looked at us apprehensively. We waved to them and they stared back as we drove slowly past.

We were now approaching the roundabout along side the Parliament Building close to the centre of town. We saw an amazing sight. There on the road part blocking the roundabout was an anti-aircraft gun, its twin barrels pointing up to the sky. Sitting astride the massive gun was a soldier wearing a red crash helmet and dark sunglasses. In his hand he clasped a Heineken beer bottle. Lying down by the side of the road were five or six ragged soldiers taunting a group of buzzards that were picking at some discarded scraps of food.

Our small convoy of cars reached the roundabout and the soldiers got to their feet and started waving their guns. As my Range Rover reached the spot where the gun was, the red helmeted soldier started winding the wheel at the side of the gun lowering the two barrels so that they were now horizontal and pointing at our vehicle. I was seated in the front alongside Vic the RMP driver and stared down the barrels of the gun which was less than a foot away. I thought to myself "I know that this window is bullet proof but I don't think that it will stop the anti-aircraft shells in that!"

I picked up the radio in the car and called up David Limb, two cars back.

"David, I think we have a bit of a problem here."

David jumped out of his land rover and strode up to the guy on the gun.

"What do you think you are doing?" he barked at the soldier. "Is this the way the new army mounts road blocks? Point that gun back up in the air."

The bemused soldier started winding the wheel and the barrels started slowly to disappear from my view seated in front of the Range Rover. Now David started shouting at the other group of soldiers. "You lot, form up here, smarten yourselves up. Where's your rifle?" he barked at a very young and very nervous soldier.

David waved us through and started drilling the group of soldiers. We edged our way gingerly past the big gun followed by the back-up land rover. I looked back with wonder and amusement at the sight of David getting this group of soldiers to come to attention and salute. I radioed David's team in the third vehicle and told them to suggest to Captain Limb that we really should be on our way and that his drill parade would have wait. David jumped into his vehicle with the group of smiling Ugandan soldiers giving him a smart salute.

We turned into Parliament Avenue where the British High Commission offices were located. We drove around the back to the American Embassy and got out of our vehicles. I knocked on the steel entrance door. The door opened furtively and the unshaven somewhat haunted face of the American Ambassador peered out. Our group was now lined up and in our hands we were holding steaming silver trays and tureens from which came the delicious aroma of roast lamb and vegetables. I looked at my colleague and announced "Lunch is served!"

After a brief chat by which time we were joined by the United Nations representative who had been in his offices in the high rise building alongside the BHC offices, we set off in our now larger convoy "to try and find out who was now running the country". We presumed that the army must have set up some form of headquarters in town but trying to find exactly where proved more difficult than we had imagined. We tried the President's Office, the Prime Minister's Office and the Ministry of Defence. They had all been ransacked but they were now deserted. A few people were sitting outside the famous Speke Hotel and others were wandering around the Nile Hotel gardens. Then as we were driving along Nile Avenue we came to the Senior Police Officers Mess and we were surrounded by soldiers. Clearly this was where things were happening.

We drove slowly through the gates with dozens of guns pointing at us. I got out of my car followed by the American Ambassador, the UN rep and a couple of our RMPs, who kept their guns by their side. We walked up to the old colonial style building. The air was electric. I started to walk along the long verandah outside the building when I spotted two figures walking towards me. They were dressed in dark suits. I recognised them. One was a friend who worked in Obote's office and the other in Alimadi, the Prime Minister's Office.

"What are you two doing here", I asked as we greeted each other with hugs.

"Oh Peter, you know we are both Acholis and therefore we have been supporting our army brothers and have been passing on information to them for a long time."

I did indeed know that they both came from Gulu in the north. I did not have a lot of dealings with them in their offices but I did used to meet them most Friday evenings at Clouds. Clouds was restaurant come nightclub which I used to go to on a Friday as a way of unwinding at the end of a hectic week. More importantly it was a favourite haunt for many of Obote's ministers and if I could not get hold of them in their offices, which was often the case, I knew that I would bump into them at Clouds usually surrounded by a retinue of mini skirted girls. I used to enjoy going up to them and saying "Ah Minister, this must be another one of your nieces whom I have not met!"

When the soldiers saw me laughing and joking with my Acholi friends, the tension eased. The soldiers put down their guns and went back to relaxing.

"So Peter, what do you want?"

I told them that my diplomatic colleagues and I wanted to find out who was now in charge.

"Oh you need to see Major Balmoi, come with us."

We walked to the end of the verandah and into the building. I was taken into a room while my colleagues were asked politely to stay outside. Inside the room I could see a group of young officers pouring over a map. They looked up, somewhat annoyed by the intrusion. My friend from the President's Office went over to the leader of the group and announced "Major Balmoi, this is the Acting British High Commissioner, Peter Penfold ... but don't worry about that, he is our friend who we meet regularly at Clouds. He wants to have a word with you."

I shook Major Balmoi's hand and he invited me to sit down. He was an impressive young man. I learned later that he was in fact the officer who had masterminded the taking of Kampala. I asked that my colleagues join us and we explained that we were responsible for our communities and that we were very concerned with the events of the past 36 hours. Many members of our communities had been attacked and robbed and were now very frightened. When would law and order be re-established? Major Balmoi listened politely. He was aware that some of his soldiers had misbehaved for which he was very sorry but things were coming under control we could reassure our communities. We chatted for a while and then left after exchanging telephone numbers which we could use to deal with any emergencies.

I dropped off my American and UN colleagues and returned to the residence without incident. I had been somewhat encouraged by my meeting with Balmoi. He clearly enjoyed the respect of the soldiers seemed to know what he was doing. We would need to have further meetings but hopefully things would begin to settle down.

They did but it took another three days before I felt it was stable enough to leave the residence and return to our homes. At the same time we organised the evacuation of 800 foreign residents which went off without a hitch; but we would not have managed it if we had not established this early contact with the new army authorities.

The short lived Okelo regime lasted six months before being consigned to history. They were driven out of office by Museveni's NRA in January 1986. The events of the weekend of 27/28 July 1985 remained in my memory much longer.

FOOTNOTE

The following letter appeared in Private Eye in September 1985 –

"Sir, Grovel's piece on Peter Penfold, acting British High Commissioner during the coup was slightly unfair. Club Clouds (not Cloud Nine) is a stuffy converted warehouse beloved of rich Ugandans trying to avoid those girls. Instead, the girls and their admittedly third rate European acolytes are to be found in a place called Chez Joseph, or at the Telex Bar, or the Speke Hotel.

In Masaka, where I live, the equivalent place is called Falkland, in honour of Maggie's great colonial epitaph.

Yours, Chris James, Uganda."

Dr Milton Obete, centre, President of Uganda, who was twice removed in military coups; first in 1971 by, on his left, Field Marshall Alhaji Dr Idi Amin Dada. On Obete's right is Bishop Kihangire.

The second time Obete was removed in a coup in 1984. Organising the evacuation of 800 members of the international community. On my right, Para Captian David Limb, left Bob Ravalico, UN Security Chief.

For Queen and Country

right: Judging the Namasagali
Annual Beauty Pageant

below: With Sandy Mobile, World
Disco Dance Champion

Heaven on Earth

The Murchison Falls, were,
in the middle of Uganda,
the River Nile is squeezed
between two rocks, 17 feet
apart.

The Miracle of Baby Heather

above: Lake Bunyoni in south-west Uganda

below: Baby Heather with left, her father, Eric Tumwesigye, and right, Dr Heather Lambert, who delivered her and in so doing saved her and her mother's life.

Climbing the snow-capped
Ruwenzori Mountains
in Uganda, the fabled
'Mountains of the Moon'.

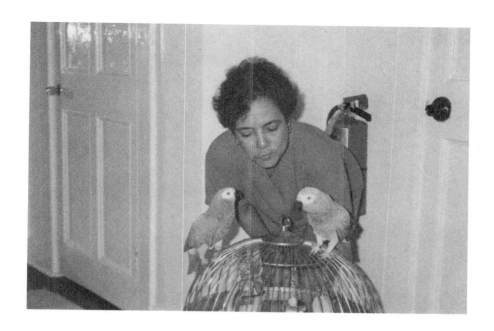

above: Parrots, Lori and
Lorito, with concerned owner
(and wife)

left: A football match in war-
torn Freetown with dynamic
No 8 Tamba Massa

Carried in a hammock through the streets of Freetown on my return from Britain and appointed as Chief.

above: Ebola in Sierra Leone – Thanking one of the burial teams

left: The late Paramount Chief Bai Kompa Bomboli II of Koya Chiefdom, in Sierra Leon

71

Chapter Twelve

HEAVEN ON EARTH

Most people's image of the River Nile is of a wide, slow flowing somewhat dirty river lined with sand and palm trees along which gallop Bedouins on horseback, as depicted in the epic film Khartoum. But in the middle of Uganda, surrounded by lush vegetation, the clear waters of this mighty African river are squeezed between two rocks just 17 feet apart and then plummet 120 feet to where crocodiles bask below, their jaws kept permanently open to catch the dazed fish who only moments earlier had been swimming sedately in the waters above. These are the Murchison Falls, in my view the most spectacular sight in the whole of Africa. Nowadays they are an easy five hours' drive from the capital, Kampala, and when you get there you are met by the sight of tourists in their tented camp in the Murchison Falls National Park, but back in the mid 1980s it was a different story.

It was 1987. We had just survived our second coup within the space of six months. President Museveni's National Resistance Army had driven the Okelo regime out of Kampala and taken over the government. After endless years of killings, misery and hardship, there was real hope that peace might finally have come at last to poor Uganda. To celebrate the peace a group of us decided to hold a "black-tie dinner" – at the Murchison Falls.

We set off from Kampala in a convoy of four diplomatic vehicles, land rovers and land cruisers, laden with our tents and camping equipment. The direct route north through Luwero and Nakasongola was still considered unsafe. The Okelo regime had been based upon the northern Acholi soldiers and groups of them were believed still to be in hiding as they made their way back north to their Acholi homeland; so we had to take a circuitous route, heading first west through Mubende and then following the shores of Lake Albert up to Masindi before striking north into the Park. The roads were not as good as they are today and it took us the best part of a day to reach Masindi, a small garrison town. One never travelled in the dark so we overnighted in a hotel in Masindi before continuing our journey the next day. We checked at the local police station in Masindi before setting off for any information about rebels in the area. We were told that there had been no incidents for a couple of weeks but the new government was still maintaining military road blocks everywhere as a precaution.

Sometimes these so called road blocks could be as unwelcoming as running into the rebels, and this proved to be the case. We were driving along the potholed road just south of the beginning of the National Park when I spotted a few twigs in the road. This was often the sign of a road block. There were no fancy well-made barriers to signify a road block. A couple of branches would be left on the road and one had to make a judgement whether they had fallen off a tree or had been purposely put there. I slowed down and signaled to the cars behind me to do so. A soldier shuffled into the middle of the road, clutching his AK 47 rifle and waved us to stop. The somewhat disheveled soldier had clearly been drinking even though it was only about 10 o'clock in the morning. He staggered up to my land rover and demanded I get out. Bitter experience had taught us all in Uganda not to argue with soldiers carrying guns, especially drunken ones. The rule was "When confronted by a soldier with a gun, wave at him and encourage him to wave back because if he is waving at you he can't fire his gun at you."

He wanted to know what we were "smuggling"(in the middle of Uganda!) I explained that we were a group of diplomats from Kampala who were going to the Murchison Falls National Park. He peered into the back of the land rover. "What's in there?" I told him that it was our camping equipment. "I need to search your vehicles".

There is no hard and fast rule on how to deal with road blocks. You just have to develop a sixth sense. Sometimes you can be officious, sometimes subservient, sometimes friendly, sometimes hostile. The main aim is to get away alive, possessions, dignity, status, are of secondary importance. I looked at my drunken friend and in a polite tone said to him "Your Army Commander, Col Tumwine, has said that you do not have to search diplomatic vehicles."

The soldier stared back at me and with all the wisdom that comes from drunkenness he replied "He may have told you that but he's not told me!"

I could not help but admire the honesty of this statement. Smiling, I put my arm around my drunken friend and said to him "You are absolutely right. The Army Commander is clearly not getting out into the field enough to meet you and our gallant soldiers who are risking their lives to keep us peace loving people safe. When I get back to Kampala I will go and see him and tell him so."

At this my friend beamed back at me and accepted the cigarette I offered him. All the while this was going four or five other soldiers were watching us from the shade of a tree. They were not as drunk as our friend but they were clearly not going to interrupt his interrogation. But once the tension had broken, they came up to our vehicles. They apologised for their drunken friend and led him away. We explained to them what we were doing and after handing out a few more cigarettes we continued on our way.

Once in the Park, the last few miles down to the Falls were especially hazardous. Only 4-wheel drive vehicles as sturdy as a land rover could make it but even so it took an hour to travel nearly two miles. We reached the Falls by mid afternoon, hot and dusty, tired and exhausted, but exhiliarated by the sight of the Falls and our journey's end. We set about unpacking the vehicles and pitching our tents. Then before commencing dinner and changing into our black tie togs and the ladies into their evening gowns, there was time to relax.

The sun was beginning to set and the air was cooled by the spray of the water. I set up my canvas chair directly in front of this spectacular sight. There was nothing man made in view to mar the sight of the magnificent falls. They were just as Sir Samuel Baker had first sighted them in 1864 and named them after Sir Roderick Murchison, President of the Royal Geographical Society at the time. Baker's etching of the Falls provides the front cover of Alan Moorhead's "The White Nile".

I reached down into my eski coolbox and pulled out one of my glass crystal tumblers. From the eski I produced some ice, no mean feat having been on the road for nearly two days. I unscrewed a bottle of Gordon's gin and opened a fresh bottle of Schweppes tonic. The fizz of the tonic splashing against the ice echoed the splash of the falls against the rocks. I was seated under the shade of a lime tree. I reached up and plucked a fresh lime and squeezed it into my drink. Blissfully content, I sipped my gin and tonic and gazed in awe at this spectacular sight of nature which God at that moment in time was displaying just for me. It was Heaven on Earth.

Chapter Thirteen

THE MIRACLE
OF BABY HEATHER

On the back of the Ugandan one hundred shilling note there used to be a picture of Lake Bunyoni, situated in the south-west of the country near to the town of Kabale and close to the Rwandan border. This whole area is full of beautiful lakes and mountains and is frequently described as "the Switzerland of Africa". I used to love visiting the area when I was serving as Deputy High Commissioner in the mid 1980s. The local people, the Bachiga, were exceptionally friendly and hard-working.

Like most Ugandans, the Bachiga had no colonial hang-ups. Many Ugandans will tell you that as a British Protectorate, unlike a British Colony, they were not colonised by the British but protected by them. In my experience, the worst colonial hang-ups came from the British, not the Africans or West Indians, and usually from those who were too young to have experiences of "the Empire". I remember visiting a Ugandan village way off the beaten track and going into the village headman's grass-roofed hut to see pictures of Her Majesty The Queen and Field Marshall Montgomery hanging side by side on the mud-brick wall.

The headman explained that before his retirement he had worked for Her Majesty; he had been a postmaster in the Royal Ugandan mail service and was very proud to have sold stamps with 'his boss's head on'! I was particularly amused to see Montgomery's picture. The headman said that he had been a member of the King's African Rifles in the Second World War and although he had not served with the illustrious Field Marshall, "General Montgomery was his favourite British General!" If this proud old man had visited Britain, how many pictures of The Queen, let alone Field Marshall Montgomery, would he have seen hanging on the walls of British homes?

Some of my friends in Kabale were very keen to maintain their links with Britain and so during one of my home leaves I went to the British Council to explore the possibility of twinning the town of Kabale with a town in Britain. At that time nearly all the twinning links were with towns in Europe, mainly France, Italy and Germany. Just by chance the town of Tiverton in Devon had approached the British Council seeking to establish a town twinning. It seemed to me that Tiverton would be an excellent partner for Kabale, both being agricultural centres in the south-west of their respective countries, so I contacted the Tiverton Town Council and suggested that they twin with Kabale. Initially they were somewhat taken aback. They had been thinking of twinning with a European town, but once they thought about it, they pursued the idea with enthusiasm and the link was established.

On one of my subsequent trips to Kabale I took with me a young lady paediatrician, Dr Heather Lambert and her partner Dr Peter Farr. Heather was at the time working in Mulago hospital in Kampala but she was originally from Tiverton.

We thought it would be fun to try and find the exact spot from where the artist had painted the picture of Lake Bunyoni on the back of the Ugandan bank note. We set off in my land rover from the Highland Hotel in Kabale, the proprietor of which was a very dear friend, Canon John Batuma, and drove for some time along rough tracks until we came to the lake. We skirted the lake and eventually found the exact spot depicted by the configuration of the lake and a large flame tree. It was very remote, no huts or people around.

There we were taking photographs of ourselves holding the hundred shilling bank note with the exact sight in the background when seemingly from out of nowhere a man came running up to us. His name was Eric Tumwesigye. "Can you help me", he said, "My wife is having a baby".

We followed him through the bush and there in a small clearing was a hut, and there in the hut was a lady obviously in an advanced state of pregnancy. We helped her into the back of my land rover and we all started to drive back to Kabale where there was a small health clinic.

It was a very bumpy ride. As we went along, the mother's water broke as we reached the outskirts of Kabale. It was a very fraught time as only the mother seemed to know where the clinic was. Between screams of labour pains she shouted instructions to me as I drone frantically around Kabale looking for the clinic. Heather was in the back taking care of the mother and by the time we reached the clinic the birth had started. It was a breach birth. As we carried the mother into the clinic, one tiny leg had already appeared from the mother's womb.

Eric Tumwesigye, Peter Farr and I paced anxiously up and down outside the clinic like three expectant fathers until after what appeared to be ages we heard the beautiful cry of a baby. What we did not know at the time was that the baby had been born not breathing and the mother had gone into a relapse. There was only one young health attendant on duty at the clinic and the complications of the birth were beyond her experience. But Heather revived them, mother and baby. She saved both their lives.

The parents named the baby girl Heather, and for her second name, because she had started to be born in my land rover with the Union Jack flying, "Nbajingo", which in the Bachiga dialect means "belongs to the British". When the Ugandan press later picked up the story, one of the journalists speculated whether the baby would have been entitled to a British passport if she had been born in the land rover!

It is now many years since that miracle occurred. The parents and Baby Heather continued to write to me to wherever I was in the world and send me photographs. In 2003 I had to visit Kampala and I hired a car and drove down to Kabale. I went round to the Bishop Kivengere Girls' High School just on the outskirts of the town where Heather was studying with her sister Rebecca. There was Heather, now 17 years old and looking very beautiful. We took photographs and I gave her some gifts and money to help with her studies. She said she wanted to become a doctor like her namesake. It was a very emotional meeting for me, and her. She later graduated from college and went on to become a fashion designer. She still stays in touch from time to time

I have often referred to this event when I have been called upon to preach. I cannot help but feel that there were just too many coincidences that day. The coincidence that we chose that day to visit Lake Bunyoni, that we just happened to be in such a remote spot, that we just happened to have a trained doctor with us. The unseen hand of God was clearly at work that day and beautiful Heather is a personification of that.

Chapter Fourteen

CLIMBING THE MOUNTAINS OF THE MOON

It was the middle of 1986. A group of us were sitting around at a party in Kampala wondering what we should do for the coming New Year. The curfew had been lifted, the drink was flowing, people were dancing to the pulsating rhythm of Billy Ocean's "Caribbean Queen"; life in Uganda was beginning to return to "normal". Most of us had experienced the two coups, the one in July of the previous year which had removed the Obote government to be followed six months later by the overthrow of the short-lived Okelo regime by President Museveni's NRA government. Life was becoming, by comparison, a little dull! What could we do to inject a little adventure into our lives? I suggested that we throw a New Year's party, in Africa, near the Equator, in the snow!

Straddling the western border of Uganda with the Congo are the Ruwenzori Mountains - the "Mountains of the Moon". They are a range of mountains stretching 70 miles in length and 30 miles in width, rising up to over 15,000 feet. The highest, Mount Stanley, reaches 16,763 feet and is the third highest mountain in the whole of Africa next to Mount Kilimanjaro in Tanzania and Mount Kenya in the neighbouring country. Although it was the ancient Egyptian geographer, Ptolemy, who first referred to the "Mountains of the Moon" as the fabled source of the River Nile, the first reliable information about the Ruwenzoris came from the famous explorer, H M Stanley, who in 1888 gazed in wonder upon the snow-capped mountain just north of the Equator which was to be given his name.

Stanley's report fired the imagination of many, including the Duke of Abruzzi, who climbed the range in 1906. For the next sixty years they attracted mountaineers and climbers from all around the world but when Uganda became embroiled in the troubles of the Amin and successive regimes, the area became too unsafe to travel in and so this incredible mountain range became abandoned and neglected.

The idea of visiting the Ruwenzoris was very appealing and we started planning the New Year adventure. I had done a little rock climbing in the UK but none of us were experienced mountaineers. We ordered climbing and camping equipment through mail order firms and, in order to get fit for this undoubtedly arduous adventure, we went walking up and down the hills of Kampala.

There were eleven of us taking part – Celia from the World Bank, Bob and Heather from Shell, Heidi (1), Claus and his wife Heidi (2), Fritz and Achim, all from the German Embassy, plus Bernd and Sonja, Claus's sister and husband who were flying in from Germany, and me. On the mountains we would be joined by three local guides, Johnson, Eric and Aloysius, and 30 porters. We set off from Kampala on Boxing Day and what follows are extracts from a log of the trip which I wrote at the time.

Friday 26 December 1986

Good weather all day

0815 We set off from Kampala only 15 minutes late which was remarkable considering how many we are and the amount of gear we are taking. Not far along the Masaka road my land rover began swaying all over the road. I thought at first it was because of all the luggage on top, including the 100 dried fish we had purchased in Nakasero market, but it turned out to be a puncture. We changed the wheel and then stopped in Masaka to repair the punctured tyre – total delay 40 minutes.

1730 We meet up with Rodney[1] on the Kasese road near Mweya lodge. She has confirmed our bookings at the Margerite Hotel and has seen John Matte[2] at Ibanda.[3]

Bob and Heather go off to the Margerite hotel to check us all in while the rest of us go straight to Ibanda to check arrangements with John Matte for setting off on the climb the next day. All the fees have gone up dramatically from what we were told back in Kampala, e.g porters from 1,000 to 3,500 (Ugandan shillings), guides from 2,000 to 7,000, blankets now cost 50,000. We sort things out and take one of our guides, Johnson, back to the hotel with us where we dine on goat stew with matoke and rice.

1030 Retire to our beds – no water in the hotel.

Saturday 27th December

0830 We set off to Kasese to buy the blankets, cassava and other food for the porters. We had previously ordered some blankets from a store in the town but when we get there it is closed. We tried another store but the woman would not budge from a figure of 55,000 per blanket, despite some persuasive talk from Celia. This is too much and we decide to offer the porters money instead of a blanket each.

The market in Kasese is closed so we stop at a smaller market on the way to Ibanda to buy 140kgs of cassava and 40kgs of meat. We wanted to buy some more dried fish but there is none available. The prices of the food are astronomical.

1130 We eventually reach Ibanda where there is chaos. Other visitors have turned up to climb the mountains, including a couple of tourists on motor bikes. Hundreds of the local Bakonjo tribesmen are hanging around wanting to be hired as porters. They are a motley group of all ages and sizes, most of them dressed in tee shirts and flip flops. Johnson selects 30 of the fitter looking ones and recommends two other guides, Eric and Aloysius, whom we appoint. We then drive up to the end of the motorised track where we park up our vehicles and start packing all our gear.

The porters are agitating. They insist that we give them their 50,000 shillings in lieu of their blankets there and then so that they can give the money to their families. We dole out 1   million shillings.

1300 We set off in good weather and good spirits, fairly arduous walking but no climbing yet.

1400 Celia slips as we are approaching the river. I grab her to stop her tumbling down the side but she has hurt her knee and after a further 20 minutes she decides to turn back – a great shame after all the preparation. She was one of the originators for the whole expedition. Johnson takes her back to Ibanda while the rest of us continue.[4]

1800 We eventually reach the Nyabitaba hut (8,700 feet), which is in a very sorry state of decay. I doubt it has been used for several years. We pitch our tents and cook a tasty meal of oxtail soup and chicken which we eat in the hut.

We retire to our beds fairly early but find it difficult to sleep. Are the effects of the altitude kicking in already?

Sunday 28th December

0730 We breakfast on cornflakes in their packets and the compo rations bacon burgers and prepare to set off but it takes over two hours before we are finally on our way.

We are following the Bukuju valley and there is a fair amount of climbing. Some of us take our time while others forge on ahead. Our long line begins to string out with Bob, Heather, Claus, Heidi (1) and me bringing up the rear. We pass through some beautiful scenery dotted with the giant lobelia plants. They are a special feature of the Ruwenzoris because of the extremes of temperature and high altitude. When immature they grow at ground level like cabbages; in adolescence they are 10 foot high mop-head palms; then suddenly they send their spectacular flowering spikes up to 25 feet into the air like giant fingers pointing to the heavens.

1530 We reach Nyamelega hut where we stop for half an hour for a quick lunch of pumperknickle, sausages and pate. As we walk alongside the river and through the trees the scenery becomes even more spectacular, almost Tolkienesque in appearance.

1630 We reach the infamous Bigo Bog, a vast expanse of swampland. Tufts of grass stick up through the swamp. In order to cross it, one attempts to jump from one tuft to another, not always successfully. The thick mud comes up to your knees. We finally reach the other side and come to the fast flowing Mubuku river which has to be crossed. There are some stepping stones but they are very slippery and I fall in the river up to my chest. Bob also falls. I change into some dry clothes on the other side and we continue on to find that Bigo Bog also extends on the other side.

1815 Our tail end group finally reaches Bigo Hut (11,300 feet), our stop for the night, very muddy and tired. Fritz and Achim are already there but worryingly not Heidi (2), Bernd or Sonja. They had been right out in front leading the line. We fire flash shells in to the darkening sky and send the two guides, Eric and Aloysius, to find our missing trio. It is now getting too dark to walk and the temperature is dropping. Heidi, Bernd and Sonja are only carrying their small knapsacks so we send two porters with Eric and Aloysius with some food, clothing and sleeping bags.

We set up our tents and cook some soup and steak which we eat in the hut. We sit around talking but everyone is concerned about Heidi, Bernd and Sonja, especially Claus, who has "lost" his wife, sister and brother in law. I stay up with Claus while the others retire to their tents. It is much colder and damper than last night, even inside the hut. Heaven knows what it must be like outside.

Monday 29th December

0730 It's a beautiful morning. The mist has cleared and for the first time we can see the snow capped mountains around us. There is no news from the guides and our strays. We cook a breakfast of sausages and baked beans and then I strip off and bathe in the nearby stream. The water is ice cold.

We cannot move on so we hang around sorting out some of our kit and wait. Some other climbers pass through our camp but they have no news of our missing people.

1415 To great relief and jubilation, Heidi eventually arrives, accompanied by Eric. She explains that she, Bernd and Sonja had taken a wrong fork in the path and had got totally lost. They retraced their steps back to the Nyabitaba hut where they spent the night huddled together under one emergency blanket. Eric and Aloysius found them that morning. Bernd and Sonja trudge into the camp about two hours later, tired and hungry.

We have an early dinner of chicken curry with savoury rice and carrots. It is very very cold and we light a fire inside the hut which quickly fills up with smoke. We have the option of freezing outside or choking inside. We open one of our bottles of champagne and sing a few songs to celebrate the wanderers' return before retiring to bed.[5]

Tuesday 30th December

0645 We have lost a whole day so we are up early. There is a thick frost everywhere, even under the portable toilet seat which I have brought with me. Every morning I set it up in an especially beautiful spot so that I can enjoy my "loo with a view!"

After breakfast of baconburgers and beans we pack up our tents and kit to set off early but it still takes a long time to get going.

0900 We climb for a while and then we descend down to the Bujuku river and across a continuation of the Bigo Bog. The scenery is beautiful surrounded by mountains, some snow capped. We come to Lake Bujuku. We skirt the lake walking through Bujuku Bog. The giant lobelias are even bigger around here. We pass Cooking Pot cave and ten minutes later we reach Bujuku Hut (13,500 feet), where we are to stop the night. We have had good weather all day which has helped us make good time. As the temperature starts to drop we set up our tents.

At the end of every day the porters come up to me with a variety of ailments. "Dr Penfold" sets up his surgery and deals with cuts, diarrhoea, and headaches. I even splint a suspected fractured toe.

Wednesday 31st December

0645 We rise early. The night was not as cold as at Bigo even though we are much higher. It's another beautiful day – we are being very lucky with the weather. I gaze upon Mount Baker in all its splendour seated upon my portable loo.

0845 After a quick breakfast of bread, ham, jam and coffee, we fold up our wet tents and set off. We are splitting up into two groups. One group (Fritz, Achim, Heidi (1), Heidi (2), Bob and myself) hopes to climb the Elena Glacier while the other group (Claus, Heather, Bernd and Sonja) will go direct to Kitandara, where we will all meet up for the New Year celebrations. The Elena group sets off first ahead of its guides who are still finishing their breakfast. We start coming across pockets of snow and, as Johnson and Eric catch up with us, we change into our warmer clothing.

1145 We reach the Elena Huts - two small triangular huts, erected in the 1950s from aluminium sheets, surrounded by snow. We are now at an altitude of just under 15,000 feet. It's an exhilarating feeling being in the snow in Africa. We spoof around for twenty minutes or so, taking photographs and putting on the wooden skis which we find in the huts.[6]

We start back as the clouds roll down and envelop the glacier. Each time the clouds clear we can see the spectacular views of the massive lobelia plants surrounded by pockets of ice and snow. We pass through the Scott Elliot Pass. Fritz, Achim and Heidi (2) have gone on ahead with Eric while our group of Bob, Heidi (1), Johnson and me bring up the rear.

As we progress down the rocky slopes in the mist, I slip badly and land on my back. Fortunately I have not sustained any serious injury but the breath is knocked out of me. After a short rest we continue.

There are two lakes at Kitandara, the upper and the lower. We skirt round the upper and as we reach the lower we spy the Kitandara Hut. Perched at an altitude of 13,200 feet overlooking the lake, it is the largest and newest of the huts in the Ruwenzori mountain range, built in 1971. Fritz, Achim and Heidi have been waiting an hour for us and just after we arrive, our other group turns up, together with two Dutch lads. We are all pretty tired and there is not much enthusiasm for a New Year's Eve party!

We all dine together on a delicious meal of goulasch (though the compo mashed potatoes were a bit of a disaster).

By 9pm we are all beginning to flake so we decide to see the New

Year in early. We uncork the three remaining bottles of champagne we have so carefully carried with us and go outside to fire the firework flares over Lake Kitandara. Many of them are damp so only two out of twenty actually light up. No matter, we wish each other Happy New Year and then go back inside the hut where we set of the party poppers I have brought. They give the hut an air of festivity and we start a sing song, switching effortlessly from songs in German and English, and Scottish. Even our Dutch friends contribute a strange song in Dutch about sharing a bath.

It's a jolly time and we keep going until around 11pm, by far the latest we have stayed up, and then we retire to our beds.

Thursday 1st January 1987

We rise around 7.15 am – good weather and beautiful surroundings. What a marvelous start to 1987! The view from my loo over Lake Kitandara is breathtaking.

After breakfast of sausages and beans we set off. We had originally planned to stop two nights at Kitandara but as we have already lost one day at Bigo we decide to move on. Today will be a hard day because we aim to get back to Ibanda in two days which means that we have to reach the Kichuchu rock shelter by tonight.

Again Heidi, Fritz and Achim set off at a good pace leaving the rest of us to follow behind in two groups – the first group comprising Heidi, Bob, Johnson and me, and then the others with Heather and Aloysius bringing up the rear – sometimes Aloysius literally brings up Heather's rear!

We climb steeply up from Kitandara and then descend over rocks to the Freshfield Pass. We had been warned that this pass was very treacherous but in the end it turned out to be merely a very steep narrow gully which we were able to negotiate fairly easily. Maybe in bad weather it is much more difficult and, as if to warn us, it starts raining. Some parts of the path which skirt the mountain are very narrow and hazardous with steep sided drops.

We trudge on in the rain. We are now very tired but finally we reach Kichuchu around 6.30pm. We are very grateful to see that the advance group has put up all our tents. The rock shelter is nothing more than the overhang of the mountain side alongside the path, which makes the huts where we have been staying seem like 4-star hotels. The ground is very boggy and there is very little room to put up our tents, let alone find a view for my loo.

We cook an easy meal of soup and sausages and retire early around 8pm, all feeling damp and exhausted.

Friday 2nd January

0730 Our final day. Luckily there is no rain as we are in a very exposed position. We set off around 9pm in our usual groupings.

The going is tough, and now made tougher with heavy rain – this is the weather that most climbers experience in the Ruwenzoris. We realise how lucky we have been. We are getting exceedingly wet and muddy but as this is our final day we are not so concerned. As we cross the Bigo Bog, we no longer worry about jumping from one tuft of grass to another, we just plow through the swamp up to our knees.

We have now completed a circular route and come back to the point where Heidi, Bernd and Sonja took the wrong fork. We pass it ominously. And then we reach Nyabitaba hut where we stop for lunch.

The rain is now torrential and the downhill climb is extremely hard on out thighs and ankles. We slide on our backsides down the steep path leading to the Mubuku river. We pass "Celia's point", the spot where she nearly fell perilously. We are now pretty tired but we start to see signs of civilisation – a few goats, the odd hut and even some people. The track becomes less muddy, our spirits are lifted and we sing a few walking songs, such as "I love to go a'wandering!"

1630 We finally reach the point where the vehicles are parked. The porters are already there. Like horses they went faster the closer they got to home. Soon all of our group has arrived and I retrieve my video camera from my land rover and capture the moments on film.[7] We take an expedition group photograph and express our sincere thanks to Johnson, Eric, Aloysius and all the porters – they were a good bunch. We pay them off, and the watchman who has been "guarding" our vehicles. He demands more money (4,500 shillings per vehicle per night!) than the hard working porters who have climbed with us up the mountains and back! We climb into our vehicles and drive off, stopping off at John Matte's house to sign the visitor's book.

We make our way to the Margerite hotel to collect Celia, who is waiting for us. We then set off for Mweya Lodge in the Queen Elizabeth Game Park where we will all relax for a couple of days before returning to Kampala. Over dinner at the Lodge we uncork our remaining bottles of champagne, which Celia has been looking after for us, and we toast the end of our great adventure.[8]

Peter Penfold

Notes

1 Rodney Richards – she was a member of staff at the British High Commission.

2 John Matte was the local agent of the old Ugandan Mountain Club.

3 The last village and starting point for climbing the Ruwenzoris from the Ugandan side.

4 Over the years the story of Celia's fall has been retold and embellished by me. What "actually happened" is that Celia had kitted herself out in all this fancy climbing gear, including a pair of very smart yellow Mephisto walking shoes which she was anxious not to get dirty! So as we were walking down this slippery muddy slope she decided to walk on the dry bracken by the side of the path. The trouble was that there was nothing under the bracken except for a 60 foot drop into the ravine below. I was walking in front of Celia when I heard the noise. As I turned around I could see her falling. I reached out and grabbed her leg. I then started to fall and the person in front of me grabbed my arm. We pulled each other up but in doing so I had wrenched Celia's knee. To this day, many, many years later, Celia, now as my wife, complains that I hurt her knee. The fact that I also saved her life gets forgotten!!

5 This incident is somewhat glossed over in my log but it could have so easily turned into an awful tragedy. There was no "mountain rescue" in the Ruwenzoris and no chance of summoning helicopters or outside assistance. With temperatures dropping to below freezing, the risk of dying from exposure was very real. We were novices and because the mountains had not been climbed for some time, the paths had become overgrown and it was very easy to get lost. After Bigo Hut we made sure that there was always one guide in front and one at the back.

6 Putting on the skis gives you honary membership of the "Ruwenzori Alpine Club".

7 There had been little point in taking my video camera up the mountains as I would not have been able to recharge the batteries.

8 For more detailed information about the Ruwenzoris, read Guy Yeoman's excellent book "Africa's Mountains of the Moon"; and if your appetite has been whetted to climb them, Osmaston and Pasteur's "Guide to the Ruwenzoris" is the definitive guide book.

Chapter Fifteen

PARROTS

One of the joys of living in Africa is that for pet lovers their choice of pet can sometimes be a little more exotic than the traditional dog, cat or hamster one has in the UK. It was not unusual for people in Africa to keep lion cubs, cheetahs, zebras, or even crocodiles and pythons. I never went that far but in Uganda, in addition to my two dogs, kept primarily as guard dogs, I had a parrot - an African Grey. He was called 'Kasuku', but in East Africa many pet lovers called their parrots 'Kasuku' as this was the Swahili name for parrot. In Britain parrots were often called 'Polly'. Maybe in olden times they were called by their Latin name, Psittacus erithacus!

Parrots are considered to be one of the most intelligent species of the animal kingdom. They are said to have the mental capacity of 2-4 year old children, and like children of that age, they can throw tantrums. If I failed to give my parrot its peanut first thing in the morning, when I went to give it to him later he would throw it back at me as if to say 'Where were you this morning?!'

Kasuku lived in an aviary that I had built around a tree on the corner of the verandah of my house in the Kampala suburb of Kololo. Parrots, African Greys in particular, are famed for acquiring a goodly selection of words and phrases and my Kasuku was no exception. He could also mimic a number of sounds, one of which was the car horn on my landrover. This would have annoying repercussions. When one approached home in your car it was common to sound the horn to warn someone inside the house to open the gate as a matter of caution. One was most at risk from being attacked whilst waiting outside your house for the gate to be opened.

At various times throughout the day Charles, my garden boy, would hear my car horn and immediately drop whatever he was doing and run up and open the gate, only to find there was no one there. Once again Charles had been deceived by Kasuku's imitation of the landrover's car horn!

Interestingly, although Kasuku fooled all of us in the house, he did not fool my two dogs, Chico and Pepe, who always seemed to know if the car horn was real or was Kasuku's mimicry. Chico was an Alsatian whom I inherited from my predecessor. He was originally called Idi but, diplomatically, this was changed to Chico. When I acquired a pup which was a mix between a Rhodesian ridgeback and a labrador, I called him Pepe. Pepe was a beautiful looking pup but like so many labradors was 'as daft as a brush'.

Pepe was always trying to join Kasuku in his aviary by burrowing under its wire fence. On many an occasion I would come home to find him lying asleep in the bottom of the aviary but with the result that the parrot had escaped through the hole made by Pepe. Kasuku was usually found in the bushes in the garden or even walking around the house.

Returning home one Sunday from an afternoon of badminton, there was Pepe in the aviary but Kasuku was nowhere to be found. I then spotted him high up a tree in my neighbour's garden. The neighbours were away so I climbed over the fence and up the tree as far as I could. Brandishing a long wooden pole I tried to entice Kasuku on to the end of it shouting repeatedly 'Get onto the pole, you stupid parrot!' He clearly thought this was some kind of game. He went to get onto the pole but then instead flew out of the tree and across to my other neighbour's compound at the end of my garden. He found another tall tree. This time there was no question of me being able to climb this tree so I had to come up with another plan to get my parrot back.

One of Kasuku's favourite pieces of music was Haydn's Toy Symphony which includes a passage of bird calls. Whenever I played this he would join in so I put the record on my record player and proceeded to blast the neighbourhood on a peaceful Sunday afternoon. Kasuku flew out of the tree and started heading towards my house. I thought I had succeeded and was feeling very happy with myself. However, he just continued flying over the roof and disappeared up into the hills behind the house. That was that; it was now getting dark and I had lost him; I was distraught.

The next morning I was having breakfast on the veranda as usual. I heard a flutter, flutter. I looked down on the ground and there was Kasuku who looked up at me and squawked 'Stupid parrot, stupid parrot'!

On completion of my tour in Uganda I left Kasuku to my successor, together with Chico and Pepe. However, Celia, whom I had met in Kampala while she was working with the World Bank, and would later become my wife, decided to take her two pet parrots with her back to the United States. So when I married Celia in the grounds of Government House, Tortola, when I was serving as the Governor of the British Virgin Islands, my new beautiful wife came with two African Grey parrots called Lori and Lorito. They became part of the family and travelled the world with us. I found it ironic having to buy plane tickets for two birds. (Couldn't we tie them to a piece of string and pull them along behind the plane?!)

Although of East African origin, when we were posted to Sierra Leone, Lori and Lorito were able to acclimatise to West Africa. They settled in their cage on the balcony of the High Commissioner's residence in Freetown to await the arrival of Celia, who would be joining me on completion of her studies at Oxford. But troubled times were afoot.

The unexpected military coup forced me to evacuate to neighbouring Guinea to join the Sierra Leone President and his government in exile. The parrots had to be left behind in the care of the residence staff. Initially it was thought that our exile would last only a matter of days or a few weeks at most. But the situation dragged on for months. This was a matter of great concern to Celia – not for her husband stuck in a hotel room in Conakry but for her parrots stuck in the residence in Freetown. Of particular concern was feeding them. All food in Freetown was scarce including parrot food. One of my activities in Guinea was to help facilitate WFP (World Food Programme) food convoys into Sierra Leone. Every now and again I managed to slip some parrot food into the convoys and get it delivered to the British High Commission.

After ten months President Kabbah's government was restored to power, the first time in Africa's history that a democratically elected civilian government removed in a coup had been restored, and Britain could be proud of the role she had played in achieving this. I returned to Freetown and to the parrots. Lorito showed his appreciation by giving me a nasty bite on my finger. Celia joined us later.

During the following months I was continually being summoned back to the UK to appear before a series of Inquiries. On one occasion while I was at our home in Abingdon Celia rang from Sierra Leone in a very disturbed state. Apparently one of the parrots had been disturbed on the balcony and flown away down the hill. Celia was in tears over the phone. What to do? I suggested that she contact one of our close Sierra Leone friends, the dynamic activist Zainab Bangura, and ask her to put out a call over the radio. An announcement was made that 'Komrabai's (my Sierra Leone Chief's name) Polly bird' was missing. A hue and cry went out and many Sierra Leoneans searched high and low for the missing parrot. Within a day Lorito had been found to the joy and relief of my wife.

Regrettably the security situation in Sierra Leone began to deteriorate again and two days before Christmas I received instructions from the

Foreign Office in London to evacuate the British community again, including the High Commission staff and families. I argued against the decision but was over-ruled although exceptionally I was permitted to remain in Freetown with my bodyguard team. When I informed Celia, who was fully engaged in making the Christmas preparations at the residence that she had to be evacuated again, she was adamant that she would not leave the parrots behind this time. (She was content to leave her husband behind!)

Most of the British community ignored the instruction to evacuate. They felt that the Foreign Office had over-reacted. Not a shot had been fired in anger. There was no sign of any rebels. So on Christmas Eve just a dozen or so members of the High Commission staff and wives and children made their way to the airport to board an RAF Hercules plane which had flown out specially. They included Celia carrying two small cages with two bemused parrots inside.

We had been told that the RAF plane would fly direct back to the UK but after it had taken off I was informed by London that the plane would only fly to Senegal further along the West African coast. Our staff in the British Embassy in Dakar were alerted to make arrangements for the Freetown evacuees, who, on arrival at Dakar were transferred to a flight to Paris, there being no flights to the UK from Senegal.

Celia duly arrived at Charles de Gaulle airport on a freezing Christmas Day morning still carrying the two parrots and dressed only in her lightweight tropical clothes. She then attempted to board a plane to Heathrow but whilst all the other evacuees boarded the flight the French officials refused to allow her to take the parrots, claiming that they would have to be quarantined either in France or the UK. This was a nonsense. Unlike most other animals, birds and parrots arriving in the UK are 'quarantined' at home where they are inspected by avian vets. Our parrots had often gone through this procedure, and Celia produced the documentation to show this. But the French authorities remained adamant; Celia could not fly on to the UK with the parrots.

Celia announced that there was no way she was going to leave her parrots to the mercy of the French authorities. If she could not fly to the UK, to where could she fly with her parrots? The French noted that the parrots had in the past transited New York so Celia was informed she could fly there – which she did, on Christmas Day flying with Lori and Lorito sitting either side of her in the near empty first class cabin. Arriving in New York the vet on duty remembered the parrots and allowed Celia to fly onto Washington where she had several friends from the time she lived there whilst working with the World Bank.

Back in Freetown I was totally unaware what had happened. I repeatedly rang our house in Abingdon but no reply. The Resident Clerk in the Foreign Office had no idea where she was. I contacted our Embassy in Dakar. They informed me that all my staff including Celia had been put on the plane to Paris. I contacted our Embassy in Paris. They made enquiries and eventually were able to inform me that Celia, plus parrots, had flown to New York. I guessed that she would fly onto Washington but by the time I spoke to one of our friends; she confirmed that Celia had indeed arrived in Washington but had now passed through to Florida where the weather would be more welcoming to an evacuee with two parrots from Africa. It would be four days since saying farewell in Freetown before I finally tracked her down and spoke to her, no thanks to the Foreign Office who were oblivious to all the distress and disruption they had caused to my wife and her parrots.

Chapter Sixteen

LIVING IN CONCRETE

When the army rebelled in May 1997 shortly after I had arrived in Freetown to take up my post as British High Commissioner to Sierra Leone, I was evacuated to neighbouring Guinea following the evacuation of 4,000 members of the international community, including 1,000 Brits, which we had coordinated. President Kabbah had earlier escaped to Guinea with members of his government and it was decided that I should remain alongside him in the capital Conakry in anticipation that we would soon return to Freetown. President Conte of Guinea accommodated his fellow President in a couple of presidential villas which had been used by two former Sierra Leone Presidents who had also fled their country. The villas were in a large compound dotted with palm trees and with camels wandering around, all set behind a 10 foot high perimeter wall. I moved into the Hotel *Camayenne* not far away. My mother back in the UK could never get her tongue around the name of the Guinean capital. She continued to tell her friends and neighbours that her son was now 'living in concrete'!

My room, number 503, in the Hotel *Camayenne* became the office of the British High Commission to Sierra Leone in exile. Running a diplomatic mission from a hotel room was not easy. Communications were especially difficult. We did receive some assistance from the local German Embassy in the spirit of European Union co-operation but generally we had to rely upon the hotel telephone and fax facilities for communication with London and elsewhere. The age of internet communication and sophisticated mobile phones had not arrived. A cumbersome satellite phone received from the Foreign Office never worked. Classified, i.e. sensitive, communication was especially difficult. The Foreign Office sent out a classified fax machine but then insisted that we keep it locked away in a security cupboard that accompanied the machine, but the cupboard was too big to fit into the hotel room and therefore both cupboard and machine had to be sent back. We stood for hours alongside the hotel's fax machine to avoid prying eyes seeing our messages going back and forth.

Staff-wise, from having run an office of over 70 members of staff, we were reduced to a 'skeleton staff'. There was an Honorary Consul in Conakry, a lovely lady, Val Treitlein, who ran the Honorary Consul's office out of her home. She was fully engaged in dealing with the normal business visitors to Guinea, exacerbated now by the flow of evacuees from Sierra Leone. Initially at the hotel I had two other UK based members of staff who had been evacuated with me but this was later reduced to just me, or when I was called back for visits to the UK, my deputy Colin Glass. The Freetown High Commission's locally engaged accountant, Brima Samura, had fled Freetown and turned up in Conakry. He was able to help out with our accounts – no easy task given that we were now operating in four different currencies: pounds sterling, US dollars, Sierra Leone leones and Guinea francs.

The only other 'member of staff' was Alphonse. He was the driver of the dilapidated taxi that I had hired on my arrival to drive me to the hotel from the airport. We kept him on paying him a generous weekly allowance. Regrettably he chose not to use this influx of funds to improve his taxi with modifications such as air conditioning or unbroken windows, let alone new tyres or brake pads. He did however buy his wife a new fridge.

However difficult life was for us in Conakry, it was far worse for the thousands of Sierra Leoneans who had fled there. For years Sierra Leoneans had looked down their noses at Guineans. De Gaulle had taken his spite out on the Guinean President, Sekou Toure, for not going along with French plans for 'controlled decolonisation' by pulling the French out of Guinea lock stock and barrel – the story went that even the telephone and electricity wires were removed. Guinea was left in a desperate state. By contrast, Sierra Leone was then a rich and developed country and Guineans came to Sierra Leone to shop and seek employment. Now the situation had been reversed and although Guinea was not rich, it enjoyed a degree of stability and development far beyond Sierra Leone's. The Guineans did not welcome the influx of Sierra Leoneans, a position exacerbated by the language difference.

The United Nations Commission for Refugees (UNHCR) had established a refugee camp in Guinea at Fourecariah near the Sierra Leone border, but many Sierra Leoneans preferred to stay in Conakry. Many of them were from the professional classes and life in a refugee camp held little attraction. However, in Conakry most of them had no homes, no jobs and no income.

Some of them managed to find menial employment and others rented shacks on the outskirts of the city. A major problem was the education of their children. They could not put them into Guinean schools so they set up their own, informally. Several of the students who fled became impromptu teachers.

A constant stream of Sierra Leoneans appeared at the Hotel *Camayenne* seeking help. I did what I could. I would invite many of them to have a meal with me in the restaurant, knowing that for some this would be the only meal they had had for days. They came from all walks of life – government ministers, teachers, students, businessmen, market women – the effect of the evacuation had been to bring everyone down to a common level. One of the most active was the civil society leader, Zainab Bangura. She was constantly organising meetings, lobbying officials and ministers, and giving interviews and press conferences, all with the aim of restoring the legitimate, democratically elected government of President Kabbah.

When we had first evacuated to Conakry we did not expect to stay more than a few days. There had been total condemnation of the coup and clearly the soldiers were finding that they had bitten off more than they could chew. However, they invited the RUF rebels who had been waging a war in the country for the past six years, to join them in Freetown and notwithstanding the continuous efforts to negotiate a peaceful solution, this led to an entrenched position being adopted by the illegal regime.

The days turned into weeks, the weeks turned into months. After the initial frenzy of the evacuation from Freetown, living in the hotel became fairly routine domestically. Deciding what to wear was no problem as all my clothes and belongings were back in Freetown. A crucial task each day was to send my one spare shirt, socks and pants to the hotel's daily laundry service. Likewise deciding what to eat was not difficult as one soon learned the restaurant's limited menu by heart and there were few alternative eating venues.

One consequence of this prolonged stay was that I missed the handing-over ceremony of Hong Kong to the Chinese government. A few years previously, when I had been serving as the Governor of the British Virgin Islands in the Caribbean, my wife and I decided that we should attend this momentous occasion in Britain's colonial history and show our support to the last Governor of Hong Kong, Chris Patten. He had succeeded me as Britain's youngest serving Governor and initially I had the idea that we should assemble all our Governors, past and present, dressed in their splendid white uniforms, swords and swan feathered bedecked pith helmets as a sign of pride and defiance to the Chinese. (Regrettably Chris Patten chose to dispense with his official uniform). We had to make our hotel booking in Hong Kong and pay for it in advance not knowing where we would be when the time came for the handing over ceremony. So when the time did come I was stuck in 'concrete' unable to move. My wife still went accompanied by her niece. I was disappointed but to make up for it I threw a party at a nearby Chinese restaurant, appropriately called the *Hong Kong* where I encouraged everyone present to wave the Union Jack and sing *Rule Britannia*.

My occupancy of Room 503 of the Hotel *Camayenne* would last altogether 276 nights. In all that time, thanks particularly to the efforts of the British Government, not one country in the world recognised the illegal AFRC junta sitting in Freetown, not even the likes of Gadaffi in Libya or Castro in Cuba. This was a remarkable example of international lobbying and diplomacy. However, as the time dragged on, we recognised that it was important that the legitimate government of President Kabbah sitting in Conakry was seen to be ready and able to resume running the country once it had returned. How to do this given the chaotic state of Kabbah's government and the fact it had no money?

Obtaining some small funding from the Overseas Development Assistance Office (ODA) of the British Government (later to be renamed DFID), I rented a run-down building which had been an Indian restaurant on one of the main thoroughfares in Conakry and stuck up a sign saying 'Government of Sierra Leone'. From there some of Kabbah's ministers were able to give the impression that they were functioning as a government.

In addition we organised a conference in London entitled 'Restoring Sierra Leone to Democracy', which was attended by a range of ministers, ambassadors and high commissioners, and addressed by President Kabbah and others such as Zainab Bangura, whose slide presentation of some of the atrocities being perpetrated by the rebels brought tears to all those in the audience. After the conference President Kabbah went on to attend the Commonwealth Heads of Government meeting in Edinburgh as the personal guest of Prime Minister Tony Blair.

The basis on which we felt confident to promote the return of the Kabbah government was not only the legitimacy of the democratic elections which had brought him to power but the will and determination shown by the Sierra Leone people who throughout all this time refused to accept the military junta as their government. It was a remarkable display of solidarity and sacrifice rarely ever seen before in the world that was to last 10 months. Thousands had fled the country but for those who remained life was extremely grim; the banks and most businesses remained closed, as were all the schools and colleges. Education is most highly prized all over Africa but the Sierra Leone students passed a resolution stating that they would stay away from classes unless and until the legitimate government was returned. When they mounted a demonstration against the junta they were gunned down by the military on the streets of Freetown.

Such stories were very inspiring to us living in Conakry as we remained in contact by phone with friends and relatives. Although food and supplies were scarce, those in Freetown would telephone telling us not to attempt to send food in as it would only be confiscated by the soldiers. When a tanker managed to get through the sanctions corridor and thus provide fuel for the city's generator and thus electric power for the residents of Freetown for the first time for weeks, instead of celebrations, I was inundated with calls from those in Freetown lambasting the international community for allowing the tanker to get through!

It was important to support the people in their struggle and encourage them not to lose hope in the face of the sacrifices they were making, especially inside the country. But how to get this message across? The junta had banned all independent newspapers and radio stations. Radio was by far the most influential sector of the media. With such a high illiteracy rate and a television service reaching just the couple of hundred sets in Freetown, it was through the radio that people were kept informed. The BBC World Service, especially its two African programmes, Network Africa and Focus on Africa, were required listening for all Sierra Leoneans. The situation in Sierra Leone dominated the African news and often the programmes carried heartfelt messages form Sierra Leoneans requesting help to rid them of the oppressive junta in Freetown.

We decided to fund a clandestine pro-democracy radio station. One of Sierra Leone's leading academics, Dr Julius Spencer, was brought back from the United States, to set it up. Radio 98.1 Democracy was an instant success. Operating initially out of a tent at Lungi Airport behind Ecomog lines, the West African force supporting the restoration of the Kabbah government, the radio broadcast to the people of Sierra Leone sixteen hours per day. It reported on the international efforts to restore the Kabbah government. Thanks to an effective network of informers in Freetown, mainly students, the station was able to report in detail on the activities of the AFRC and RUF, highlighting their crimes and misdeeds.

Radio 98.1 really got up the noses of the junta. No sooner had they held a meeting among themselves, than details of what had been discussed were being broadcast to the people. The junta was continually trying to discover from where the radio station was broadcasting. They warned people not to listen to it. One 80 year old woman was killed for just doing so. Radio 98.1 became the main source of information to the Sierra Leone people about what was going on in their country. It was a source of much strength and encouragement to the residents of Freetown, who went to bed with their radios beneath their pillows to dampen the reception, listening to Spencer and his colleagues.

We deliberately did not publicise our support for Radio 98.1 for fear of reprisals being taken against our staff and properties, but from time to time I would give a live interview by telephone from my hotel room in Conakry in which I encouraged the people to keep faith with democracy and not to lose hope. Because of these interviews and my other activities, I became one of the 'enemies of the AFRC revolution' I featured on the RUF's 'hit list'. When it was incorrectly reported that I had been replaced as British High Commissioner, *We Yone*, the pro junta newspaper, produced an editorial headed 'Good Riddance to Penfold'.

We did finally return to Freetown thanks to the efforts of the West African military force, Ecomog, led by Nigeria. I sailed back in style aboard a British warship, HMS Cornwall, taking with us the Sierra Leone Foreign Minister, Shirley Gbujama. A week or so later President Kabbah returned to a hero's welcome; the first time in Africa's history that a democratically elected head of state removed in a military coup had been returned to power.

Chapter Seventeen

A FOOTBALL MATCH

The eleven year rebel war in Sierra Leone witnessed some of the most appalling atrocities in Africa's tormented history. Most of the atrocities had occurred outside of Freetown as the RUF (Revolutionary United Front) rebels led by the megalomaniac Foday Sankoh, waged their campaign of terror, mutilation and destruction in the rural areas. But for the people living in the capital, hitherto generally spared from these atrocities, the 6th of January 1999 will be the day that long remains in their memories. On that day the rebels launched their attack on the capital. In the space of 10 days, 7,000 people were brutally murdered, hundreds had their hands and legs hacked off, thousands of women and children were raped, a third of the population were forced to flee their homes and half of the city was systematically destroyed.

At the time I was not in Freetown. Initially I had refused to join the evacuation of the British community called for by the Foreign Office on the Christmas Eve believing that it would precipitate the attack by the rebels, but after attending peace talks in Abidjan, the capital of the Ivory Coast at the end of December, I was refused permission to return to Freetown. I went to neighbouring Conakry, the place where I had spent 10 months after the May 1997 coup, and from where I followed the awful events taking place in Freetown.

By the end of January I was allowed to move on board a Royal Naval warship, which had been stationed off the Sierra Leone coast. I started commuting daily by helicopter or rubber boat into the war devastated city; however the commuting lasted only a few days because, after coming under "friendly fire" from the Ecowas forces who were guarding the Aberdeen bridge, we considered it was actually safer to stay ashore in Freetown.

By now most of the rebels had now been driven out of the capital and a degree of peace had been restored, but there were thousands of displaced people all around the city, including about 20,000 camped out in the National stadium, because they had no homes to go back to. They had been destroyed. I visited the stadium regularly and gave what help I could. The conditions were awful. No electricity, no running water, limited amounts of food either donated by NGOs or scavenged around the town, and appalling sanitary conditions. It was difficult to recall that less than ten months previously this had been the scene of intense jubilation when thousands of Sierra Leoneans had welcomed back their President, Tejan Kabbah, flanked by Sani Abacha and Lansanna Conte, the Presidents respectively of Nigeria and Guinea, whose troops had ousted the illegal junta of Johnny Paul Koroma. I had been there on that famous day; now the atmosphere in the stadium was much more subdued.

One of the stadium toilets had been designated 'the maternity ward' to cope with the never ceasing succession of births with such a large gathering of people. It was run by a couple of Sierra Leonean midwives, who had also been made homeless by the rebels. I was full of admiration for these heroic 'Florence Nightingales' valiantly trying to cope under the most appalling conditions. On one of my visits I watched them help a young mother give birth to a child on the toilet floor. It was pitiful. There was not even a rag to wrap the baby up in. (To add to the child's woes the family decided to name the baby 'Peter Penfold Amara'.) I recounted this sight to some close friends in Cardiff and, unbeknown to me, they copied my letter to others in and around Cardiff. One month later I received 22 sack-loads of baby clothes – yet another example of the amazing generosity of people in Britain to respond in times trouble. I distributed the clothes to those in need in the various displaced camps around the capital.

The National Stadium had been built by the Chinese in the 1970s. In its day it had been a splendid building but it was now showing signs of decay after years of neglect. Inside the displaced families marked out their spots on the cold concrete floors underneath the stands and around the outside of the building. Day after day they sat there in the wretched conditions with the few possessions which they had managed to carry as they fled from the attacking rebels. It was a depressing sight.

The middle of the stadium was deserted as this did not provide any protection from the sun. Therefore the grass on the football pitch, though somewhat dry from the sun, was in relatively good shape. This led me to come up with what some initially considered a crazy idea.

I suggested to the "committee" which had been set up by those in the stadium to oversee conditions that we arrange a football match between those in the stadium and the Royal Navy ship, HMS Westminster. It is common during a ship's visit to arrange a local football match and although there were clearly other things to do, why not? I said that I would kit out the team with the assistance of the ship and I asked the committee at the stadium to select a team. This led to much excitement. The search to pick their strongest team became as intense as if they were choosing a team to play in the World Cup. This was to be Sierra Leone versus England. They called themselves the 'Displaced Stars XI'.

The day came for the match. Decked out in their blue and white striped shirts, which I had managed to acquire, (I had deliberately chosen Chelsea's colours!), the Displaced Stars XI took to the field to the cheers of the thousands gathered in the stadium, including the Minister for Sports, The Hon Dr Alpha Wurie, as the guest of honour. HMS Westminster's XI looked decidedly fitter and better nourished.

The two teams were introduced to the Minister and me and the National Anthems were sung. Then the referee blew his whistle and the match kicked off. HMS Westminster took an early lead. But, urged on by their supporters, the Displaced Stars fought back and soon they had equalised. One of their players, their No 8, a young man called Tamba Massa, put on a virtuoso performance. He was only half the size of the other players on the pitch, but the crowd went wild as he weaved in and out of the legs of the opposing team.

The game went on in the hot sun and the sailors began to wilt. The Displaced Stars scored, and scored again. The enthusiasm of the Sierra Leone team was matched by the excitement of the spectators. Finally the referee blew his whistle to signal the end of the match. The Displaced Stars had won 5 -1.

The crowd was ecstatic. I looked around at their smiling faces. For just a short couple of hours, all the miseries and turmoil that they had faced, and continued to face, in those wretched conditions were forgotten as they cheered their team off the pitch. It was a special moment, a reminiscence I will never forget.

Chapter Eighteen

PARAMOUNT CHIEF

By the fifteenth century Sierra Leone was divided into numerous small kingdoms that were governed by a collection of warriors, hunters or traders. Titled 'owners of the land', they exercised complete authority within their domains. In 1896 the British declared the interior of Sierra Leone a Protectorate, while Freetown and the peninsular were declared a colony. They designated the rulers in the Protectorate 'paramount chiefs' and presented each with an official symbol of office – a cane staff topped with a brass knob bearing the British coat of arms. Although the paramount chief was still the highest ranking personage of his domain, he had to share the powers of leadership with a British district commissioner who oversaw several chiefdoms. A paramount chief primarily kept law and order and collected taxes. He also recruited labour for projects such as building roads. The district commissioner retained responsibility for settling land disputes and judging criminal cases. This was the system of 'indirect rule' by which Britain exercised her colonial authority in Sierra Leone and in many other parts of the Empire.

At the time that I was British High Commissioner there were 149 paramount chiefs spread throughout Sierra Leone. Many of them could trace their lineage back to the original chiefs and rulers. Twelve chiefs, one from each national district, sat in the national Parliament, like a mini House of Lords within the House of Commons. The chiefs were the real power and influence in the country. Governments come and go, but the chiefs provided the continuity of authority. They were the persons to whom the people turned for advice and guidance. They ruled their people but they were also answerable to them. If the people were not satisfied with the performance of their chief, he, or she, (there were some lady paramount chiefs but only in the south) would be removed. So although they represented an ancient traditional system of authority, they were also part of a modern democratic system of government. Because of the chiefs' immense influence several of them had been brutally killed during the rebel war and many others had to flee their chiefdoms.

Since independence in 1961 The Queen and Prince Philip had been the only non-Sierra Leoneans to be appointed paramount chiefs; but this was about to change.

Conakry Airport was as chaotic as ever as I disembarked from the plane returning from London where I had been facing the interrogation of the Legg Inquiry looking into the 'Arms to Africa/Sandline Scandal'. Guinean health official demanded to see everyone's certificates against smallpox, yellow fever, cholera and then to reach the exit you had to run the gauntlet of dozens of customs officials, each one wanting to inspect every piece of baggage. Alphonse, the Guinean taxi driver whom we had employed as our official driver during our exile in Guinea, was on hand to meet me and we drove the familiar route through the bustling streets of Conakry in the half-light of early evening to the Hotel Camayenne. Room 503, the room which I had occupied during our exile, was not available but I was given room 403 immediately below it, so everything seemed identical to what had been so familiar for those ten long months. I took a shower, phoned Celia and then watched a movie on the French TV channel before falling asleep.

Alphonse came back to pick me up in his dilapidated taxi the next morning. He asked to borrow some money- another piece of his taxi had fallen off. We drove out to the airport where I was joined by Desmond Luke, who was now Chief Justice, and Charles Margai, the Minister of Internal Affairs. They said they had been delegated to accompany me back to Freetown. Instead of flying as normal to the international airport at Lungi, our charter plane flew directly to Hastings, the old airport on the outskirts of the capital.

As the plane landed and taxied round in front of the wooden huts that represented the terminal, I looked out through the window and could see a crowd gathered. I stepped off the plane and was immediately surrounded by cheering Sierra Leoneans. Drums were banging and there was lively singing from a group of women in their white and green dresses. I was escorted to the terminal building. A number of familiar faces were around.

I was introduced to King Naimbana II, the Temne tribal chief. He sat me in a chair and announced to everyone that I was to be made a paramount chief. He produced a traditional costume made out of bark cloth and proceeded to put it over my head. He place a hat made of the same material on my head. A pair of trousers were also produced but we agreed that it would not be dignified for me to drop my pants in front of the assembled crowd so I handed them to Mal, head of my close protection team, who was on hand. Television cameras were catching the events. King Naimbana delivered a little speech and handed me my staff of office – a wooden stave with a brass knob. I was led back outside to the singing and dancing. I went up to the drummers and singing women and started to dance with them. This brought more loud cheers. I was then led to my land rover and climbed inside.

A long line of cars both preceded and followed us into Freetown. Apparently the ceremonies were still not over. With horns blaring and people waving and shouting we entered the city limits. Bunches of schoolchildren bedecked in their smart school uniforms lined the route and waved as we went past. As we came up to the PZ roundabout the crowds got thicker. The vehicles stopped and I alighted from the vehicle. I was led over to a hammock made of rope with a wooden awning perched over the top of it, painted in red, white and blue on the outside and blue, white and green, the colours of the Sierra Leone national flag, on the inside. On the front of the awning in bold white lettering was written 'Sierra Leone welcomes back HE Peter Penfold'. The whole structure, which must have been considerably heavy, was supported on the heads of four strong Sierra Leoneans.

I was lifted bodily into the hammock and we started to process along the street surrounded by hundreds of smiling and cheering Sierra Leoneans. Most of them were waving home-made Union Jacks and Sierra Leone flags, which obviously they had all made the night before in their homes in preparation for the day's festivities. Being carried in a hammock is the traditional mode of transport for a paramount chief, but it was not easy. I had never been briefed on how one travels by hammock. Did I stretch my legs out or let them hang either side? I tried to sit up as we proceeded uphill so that I could see what was going on. One woman followed alongside me, fanning me with something that looked like a large table mat made out of straw. Every now and then her hand slipped and I would receive a nasty whack on the back of my neck. Immediately behind the hammock came Paul, one of the close protection team. Quite what he would be able to do to protect me in such a large crowd, I had no idea, nor, did I guess, did he.

The route was lined with Sierra Leoneans of all ages cheering and waving. I waved back. We went along Siaka Stevens Street. What the late President, who had declared Sierra Leone a republic in 1971, would have made of all this, I dared to think. Here was I, a white man, a representative of the former colonial power, being carried in a hammock through the streets of the capital of this African country nearly forty years after independence. Probably more Union Jacks were being waved than at any time during the height of Queen Victoria's empire.

The procession continued until we reached the Cotton Tree, the symbol of Sierra Leone in the centre of Freetown, where in the olden days the freed slaves would gather. I was lifted out of the hammock and carried to the steps of the Law Courts building. The crowd was now a couple of thousand strong. Before mounting the steps I went back to the hammock to shake the hands of the four porters who were sweating profusely. I then went up the steps of the building and was seated in front of the cheering crowd. Behind me sat a number of VIPs on white plastic chairs.

King Naimbana came to the microphone and announced that I had been made a paramount chief and that henceforth I was to be known as Paramount Chief Komrabai Peter Penfold. Moslem and Christian prayers were said and other speeches were made. I was then invited to speak. I started by saying 'am gladdie tbe bak een me oon hoos' the Krio for 'I'm pleased to be back home.' The crowd cheered. I said I was honoured to become a paramount chief, an honour which I accepted on behalf of Her Majesty The Queen, the British Government and the British people. I noted the commitment of the Sierra Leone people to democracy and the sacrifices they had made to keep it. I promised them the continued support of the British Government and people. There were more loud cheers and singing. After another speech it was finally time to get back into the vehicles. Again I was surrounded by the seething masses all wanting to shake my hand. We made it to the land-rover and slowly drove away past the American Embassy and Nigerian High Commission, up the hill, to Runnymede, the British High Commissioner's residence.

The next day in the office I had to send a telegram reporting on my return as instructed. There were already too many people back in the UK who believed that I had 'gone native', so I tried to keep the report light-hearted. I sought instructions on what was the official mileage rate for travel by hammock and asked how many porters I was entitled to. I suggested that close protection teams would require training drills on how to escort a hammock-travelling High Commissioner. One aspect of the appointment sounded interesting. I was told that a paramount chief was entitled to ten wives. I sought advice whether my allowances would be increased to reflect this. I mentioned this fact to my wife. As my number one wife it was her duty to help select the other nine for me. I'm still waiting!

Although I had played down my appointment as a paramount chief to London, in Sierra Leone it was taken seriously. The number of people wanting to see me trebled and I received half a dozen letters a day seeking favours and requests such as for a job or money, food , clothing, or frequently asking me to intercede in a dispute. As I did not have a designated chiefdom, it was felt that all and sundry could approach me. Also, because I had been given the title 'Komrabai', which means 'elder of the chiefs', many of the chiefs themselves would approach me for advice and assistance.

I remain immensely honoured to have been made a paramount chief in Sierra Leone. It undoubtedly helped me do my job as High Commissioner. As a paramount chief I was entitled to direct access to the President at all times; President Kabbah took to calling me 'Chief' instead of 'Your Excellency'. All doors of power and authority were open to me. I especially developed close relationships with some of my fellow paramount chiefs around the country which remain to this day.

One of those Chiefs with whom I developed an especially close relationship was Paramount Chief Bai Kompa Bomboli II of Koya Chiefdom. In his 90s he was the longest serving Paramount Chief in the country. Based in Masiaka, 50 miles outside the capital, Freetown, the town is the gateway to both the north and the south of the country. As such it suffered much during the 11 year rebel war. I took the British Minister Clare Short to Masiaka on both her visits to Sierra Leone to show her the extent of the destruction of the war. The first time there were barely a few hundred people still living in the town of once 15,000 inhabitants and there was not even a chair on which the Minister could sit! We took Chief Kompa with us. He had had to flee for his life when the rebels over-ran the town and was living in Freetown. He announced to his people that he would be returning shortly. As a result, when Clare Short paid a second visit 8 months later, thousands had returned from the capital and the surrounding bush and there were plenty of chairs to sit on. This demonstrated to the Minister that a key to getting the country back on its feet was to get the Chiefs back to their chiefdoms and so she allocated some British aid funds to help rebuild the Chiefs' houses and the Court Barres, the traditional chiefdom meeting places.

Another person I took to meet Chief Kompa was my godson, Jack Latham. His first time in Africa, he found it a daunting experience. Mischievously I persuaded him that it would be customary for him to present the Chief with a gift. Accordingly, rather nervously, he presented Chief Kompa with a pineapple that we had bought along the roadside on the way to Masiaka. Unbeknown to Jack, the Chief had his own large pineapple plantation behind his house. With a twinkle in his eye Chief Kompa graciously accepted the gift. It became a joke between the Chief and me for years to come. Jack has gone on to become one of Britain's leading photographers as a direct result of his visit to Sierra Leone, and his portrait photograph of Chief Kompa Bomboli hung proudly in the Chief's parlour. Sadly the Chief has now died but his legacy and the photograph live on.

The accepted form of greeting from one paramount chief to another is

'My Good Friend'. A few years ago when Tony Blair on a visit to Sierra Leone was made a paramount chief of a village near the airport. I sent him a letter of congratulations addressed to 'My Good Friend'. He did not reply!

Chapter Nineteen

A SONG FOR SALONE

I grew up in the 1950s in Brixton in south London and then at the age of nine we moved to a large Council Housing estate in Surrey. They were enjoyable times, in which music played an important part. My "pop idol" was Buddy Holly, but I was also caught up in the skiffle craze which swept Britain. Lonnie Donegan was "the King of Skiffle" and, like thousands of other teenagers at the time, I got hold of a second-hand guitar. Having mastered just three chords I would unembarrassingly display my meagre talents at youth clubs and scout camp fires. It was great fun for me, less so for the audiences. Skiffle gave way to folk singing as four of us formed a folk group singing Peter, Paul and Mary and Kingston Trio songs. On one memorable occasion we performed at the South Wimbledon Deaf and Dumb club. It amused me to think that half of the audience could not hear our singing and the other half could not say whether they liked it or not!

After I had joined the Foreign Service, my guitar accompanied me on my diplomatic postings around the world and as well as occasionally inflicting my noise on guests at parties, I would compose the odd song. In Kampala I wrote a song about Uganda – "Uganda My African Home". I was flattered when it was recorded by one of Uganda's leading entertainers – Jimmy Katumba. Indeed Jimmy and his group, the Ebonies, actually put on a concert to mark my farewell from Uganda – a rare honour. I continued the habit by writing another song when I was Governor of the British Virgin Islands – "Caribbean Christmas", which I would perform with the local brownies at the annual Christmas concert at Government House.

But probably my most noted composition was the song which I wrote for Sierra Leone – "My West African Home". I recorded it with the choir from the Milton Margai School for the Blind in Freetown to help raise funds for the school and I had the privilege of singing it with the choir when they toured Britain in 2003, including at an inspirational concert at Westminster Abbey.

The words were written to reflect my deep commitment and love for the country and people of this poor West African country which had suffered so much in recent times. They are as follows:-

"No more guns, no more killing,
No more crying or fear of living.
No more hunger, no more pain,
No more hiding in the rain.
Peace and democracy,
That is what we want to see,
Here in Salone, Si-erra Leone,
Where ever you roam,
In this, my West African Home.

Temne, Mende, Limba, Krio,
Susu, Fula and Mandingo.
Black and white, rich and poor,
Young and old, big and small.
Deaf and dumb, blind or lame,
Moslem, Christian,
We're all the same.
Here in Salone, etc

Throughout this land, where 'ere you go,
From north in Makeni to south in Bo.
Head east to Kenema or Kailahun,
Or go to Kono or Pujehun.
On ev'ry trip, along ev'ry mile,
You'll find a wave and a friendly smile,
Here in Salone, etc."

When I first wrote the words, the town of Kono was not mentioned in the lyrics. Shortly after writing the song, I tried it out with a group of friends which included my driver and traveling companion, Emmanuel Fillie, when we were relaxing at a beach side restaurant just outside Freetown. I asked Emmanuel what he thought of it. Although he said he liked it, I could see that something was bothering him.

"What's the matter, Emmanuel?" I asked him.

"But High Commissioner, you have not mentioned my home town."Emmanuel comes from Kono, the diamond mining area in the north of the country, which suffered a great deal during the rebel war - so "Kono" was inserted into the lyrics!

Emmanuel would keep a taped copy of the song in the official car and on one occasion he played it to Clare Short, the visiting Secretary of State for International Development, when we were driving to Masiaka, one of the most war devastated towns in Sierra Leone. Clare Short has a naughty sense of humour and when she came to the end of her speech to the large crowd assembled in Masiaka to listen to her, she announced to them: "And now we will get our High Commissioner and your Paramount Chief to sing the song which he has written about Sierra Leone." With Emmanuel's copy of the tape playing in a tape recorder borrowed from one of the accompanying journalists and singing through a loudhailer supplied for the occasion, Clare Short and I gave an impromptu rendition of "My West African Home"!

Several years later Lord Richards, former Chief of the Defence Staff, appeared as a guest on the long-running radio programme Desert Island Discs. As Brigadier David Richards he had masterminded the British military involvement which helped finally bring an end to the rebel war in Sierra Leone. He was a hero to the Sierra Leone people and I admired him greatly. Working together we had become close friends. For one of his eight chosen pieces of music for the programme, he selected 'My West African Home' sung by the choir of the Milton Margai School for the Blind with soloist one High Commissioner Peter Penfold. Indeed David identified this disc as the most cherished of the eight selections. I was very flattered.

Chapter Twenty

EBOLA

I am writing some of these anecdotes in the Spring of 2020 when the country is in the grip of the corona virus crisis and I am confined to my home in self isolation. The corona virus has ravaged the world, staring in China, the epi-centre moved to Europe and decimated populations in Italy, Spain, and now the UK where as I write this the death toll is approaching 10,000 with still no end in sight.

One interesting aspect of this crisis is that so far it would appear that Africa has been spared the worst of the effects. No one can be exactly certain why but it has been a novel experience for me to have friends in Sierra Leone ringing me to check that I am OK, a great contrast to times past where I was always ringing them in Sierra Leone to check on them.

Five years ago it would be to check on how they were coping with the ebola pandemic. There are many similar features between the ebola and co-rona viruses. Both spread like wild fire and both are extremely deadly. Over a 2 year period between 2014 and 2016 there were 28,600 cases of ebola in the three West African countries of Guinea, Sierra Leone and Liberia including 11, 325 deaths, of which nearly 4,000 were in Sierra Leone. Although scien-tists all around the world are presently focusing their attention on finding a vaccine to stop COVID 19, it is salutary to note that we still have not discov-ered a vaccine against ebola even though it has continued to re-occur in the Congo, where it first started.

I visited Sierra Leone a couple of times during the ebola crisis to show my support. What follows are a couple of articles which I wrote at the time.

I have now been here two weeks. During my last visit in April the first cases of ebola had appeared. Deaths had been reported in Sierra Leone and before that in the neighboring countries of Guinea and Liberia. Only MSF (Medicins Sans Frontieres) were warning of the seriousness of the outbreak but at the time no one was heeding the warnings, neither the local governments nor the international community. Since then the ebola virus has ravaged this part of West Africa. There have been nearly 21,000 reported cases and over 8,000 reported deaths.

Disgracefully but sadly not surprisingly, it took a couple of incidents affecting the UK, US and Spain before the rest of the world woke up to the danger and help started to arrive in sufficient numbers financially and logistically. Now, as numbers in Guinea and Liberia appear to be tailing off, here in Sierra Leone numbers continue to rise, albeit at a slower rate. As at the beginning of the year there had been 9,700 cases and 2,557 deaths, including 221 health care workers, who are in the forefront of the efforts to combat the deadly disease.

I visit Sierra Leone regularly two or three times a year. Compared to my previous visits there are a number of tell-tale signs to indicate that this is now an 'ebola country'. Immediately upon arrival at the airport one is subjected to having your temperature taken and the washing of hands in chlorine water. When I was here during the rebel war in the late 1990s one was used to seeing young men going around carrying guns. Now the AK47s have been replaced by 'temperature guns' which fire laser beams at your forehead to give temperature readings. (One of the early signs of ebola is high fever, although, of course, the readings cannot distinguish between ebola fever or malaria and all the other numerous prevalent ailments that can lead to high temperatures). Such checks are carried out by teams of workers as one enters any building, e.g. hotels, restaurants, banks, offices, etc, and at improvised road blocks.

Another obvious tell-tale sign emanates from the 'no touch' policy; perhaps not so apparent to the first-time visitors from Britain where the practice of hugging and embracing in public is not so widespread. But here in Sierra Leone this is how one greeted friends and acquaintances. I made a mistake on arrival. Spotting an acquaintance at the airport, I was immediately hugging them before I was reminded, politely, that this was no longer done. I have had to get used to nodding one's head or tapping your heart with one's fist.

The influx of personnel from the international agencies and NGOs is very apparent. Many more white faces and scores of white four-wheel drive vehicles emblazoned with their distinctive logos of the Red Cross, SCF, UN, etc drive around, going past the multitude of posters and billboards warning of the dangers of ebola. And then there's the 'frontline' vehicles – the ambulances and burial vans. In one day I can see more ambulances than in a whole month on previous visits; and the burial vans, at first seemingly innocuous looking like the regular 'poda poda' transport buses, (indeed until recently that's what they were); but the covered windows and the absence of any number plates are the give-away that these vehicles have a different purpose, going to or carrying away the bodies of the dead ebola victims to put them in the overflowing cemeteries.

Less apparent unless one goes looking for them are the various ebola treatment centres dotted around, some in schools and old buildings, others purpose built such as that at the British built and funded Kerry Town centre on the outskirts of Freetown.

Other than these tell-tale signs, life can appear as normal. Freetown is as crowded and bustling as ever with people walking around, shopping in the busy open air markets, chatting on the sidewalks. One significant difference, however, is the total absence of any school children. The children are around but hitherto it was such a common sight to see the thousands of schoolchildren in their identifiable smart colourful school uniforms walking to and from their schools. Now all the schools are closed.

Some attempts have been made by the government to replace school attendance with teaching lessons on radio and television but these are not available to all throughout the country. The impact of this loss of formal education upon the present youth generation could be incalculable, although government should be extremely wary of rushing the re-opening of schools. Younger children, more than most, find the 'no touch' policy difficult to follow, as I witnessed at church on my first Sunday here. There is a risk that one ebola case could affect a whole school.

Of an evening the city takes on a different feel. From 6 o'clock all shops and bars and restaurants close. People are banned from congregating in large groups. Only the bars and restaurants of some of the larger hotels remain open, mainly for the benefit of their occupants and providing some relaxation for the numerous hard-working international personnel and visiting media. Most Sierra Leoneans just stay at home.

My wife and I usually come every year to welcome in the New Year in Sierra Leone. This year my wife remained in the UK and for me the New Year arrived unnoticed – no parties, no fireworks, no gathering on the Lumley Beach. The profoundly religious people of Sierra Leone were permitted to go to churches and mosques for early services but had to return to their homes immediately afterwards. As with the Christmas festivities a few days earlier, there were no celebrations. In effect, Christmas and New Year were cancelled this year in Sierra Leone.

Ebola now dominates the life of Sierra Leone. Virtually every TV, radio or newspaper item is ebola related, whether it's reporting the latest deaths, the handing out of much needed assistance to the victims, the innumerable ebola meetings and conferences or the endless visits from overseas dignatories such as the UN Secretary-General, African Presidents, US Vice President, British Ministers and ex-Prime Ministers. Where before, most Sierra Leoneans followed every football score of the UK premiership, now they can recite the daily scores of new ebola cases and new deaths from all around the country.

After a slow start, the UK now leads the international assistance in combatting the virus and the British effort, led by the dozens of dedicated, voluntary doctors and health care workers has made and continues to make a big difference. The decision by the British government to suspend direct air flights is the one blot on these efforts. Not only is it not helping the arrival of supplies and personnel, it leaves a somewhat sour taste in the mouths of Sierra Leoneans who feel they are being stigmatized by the country with whom they have such a close relationship.

Ebola dominates the economy. With the closing down of businesses and the laying off of staff, practically the only jobs available are ebola related, whether it is working in the treatment centres, manning the telephone hotline, members of the courageous burial teams, grave diggers, drivers for the ebola agencies and NGOs – all of them funded by the huge influx of funds from overseas (around £350 million and growing).

There are some cautiously optimistic signs that this concerted effort is beginning to see the tide turning. As the cases are reported more speedily and those affected taken earlier to the treatment centres, there are increasing numbers of people recovering and becoming 'ebola free'. They are the victors in this war though the threat of stigmatization remains. Many still find it difficult to be accepted back into their communities. Safer burials are having a marked impact. Some parts of the country, e.g. in the south and east, are seeing low of nil new cases of ebola; however, other areas, e.g. in the diamond mining areas around Kono, continue to see numbers rising. In such areas it has proved so difficult to persuade people to abandon their culture and traditions of touching and washing dead bodies, the single most significant cause of spreading the disease. In one instance alone, one ebola case led to a further 36 people being affected. The role of the Paramount Chiefs in getting the anti-ebola messages across to the people has been crucial. Regrettably it took some time for the government and outside agencies to recognise this. Initially politicians were used for the public education programmes, but Sierra Leoneans, like most people around the world, find it difficult to always believe what a politician says!

Much hope has been placed upon the frantic search to find a vaccine cure and there are some encouraging developments; but most experts doubt that we will see suitable vaccines in sufficient numbers before the end of the year. Why it has taken the world so long to focus its energies on finding a vaccine for a deadly virus which has been around since 1976 is one of the big questions which the 'experts' will ponder in the no doubt countless reports that will emerge after the crisis is over?

Notwithstanding the positive signs, we cannot afford to become complacent. Sierra Leone will probably continue to live with the ebola threat at least until the end of the year, albeit much reduced. However, already people are asking what happens after ebola? The last ebola case (if such a situation arises) will leave behind a devastated country once again, just as we experienced at the end of the 11 year rebel war. It took years to recover from that, but progress was being made. At the start of 2014 the GDP was growing at 14%, one of the highest in Africa. The Minister of Finance now predicts growth at 4%, and may people fee is being unduly optimistic. It is not just the health sector which has been destroyed, (not that it was up to much before ebola,) but all sectors of the country's development have been decimated – education, employment, infrastructure, agriculture. Sierra Leone was, and potentially always will be, a rich country, the mainstay of which is its agriculture. A country which could feed itself and export crops, and yet now some experts are predicting a famine in Sierra Leone this year because farmers have not been able to plant their crops.

One hopes that when this ebola country is ebola free, the world will not think that the job is finished. It may be then that the most help will be needed to get this beautiful country full of courageous people back on its feet.

EBOLA IN SIERRA LEONE – PART 2

The number of ebola deaths in Sierra Leone has now risen to over 3,000. WHO reports that as of 14 January there have been, a total of 10,124 ebola cases and 3,062 deaths.

Approaching my fourth week in Sierra Leone, I have been able to travel more widely around the country. I went 'upline' to Bo, Sierra Leone's second city, (or is that now Makeni with the northern based APC government in power?), and into the surrounding Chiefdoms. Life in the south appears more relaxed than in Freetown and the Western area.

Having gone more than 42 days without any new cases, Pujehun District has been declared 'ebola free' and the neighboring districts of Bo, Kenema, and Kailahun also report low incidence. Precautions are still in place – you still get fired upon with the temperature guns at numerous road blocks and encouraged to wash your hands with chlorine water, but in Bo town, for example, the checks are not as rigid as in Freetown. However, there is still the need not to become complacent and to remain vigilant, as vividly demonstrated with the sad death this week of yet another Sierra Leone nurse in Kenema. Meeting and thanking one of the courageous burial teams outside the Bo hospital has been one of the most satisfying events of my trip.

On the main highways there is the usual sight of people selling their charcoal and crops such as pineapples, oranges and pawpaw and drying their rice by the side of the road but not as much as before. Driving into the rural areas, life appears even more normal with only cursory ebola checks at roadblocks into the bigger villages. Visiting our agricultural project deep into Lugbu Chiefdom, it was encouraging to see rice and groundnuts being grown, but we still insist that our workers wash their hands with chlorine water and carry out temperature checks Elsewhere in the south farming is taking place though not as widespread as one would expect at this time of year before the rains come. We deliberately started up our Lion Mountains Agrico project two months ago to emphasise the need to get agriculture going in the country in the face of predicted food shortages.

The closer to Freetown the more vigorous are the road checks manned by police and army leading to long lines of trucks and buses. Having an ebola vehicle pass issued by the NERC (National Ebola Response Centre) in Freetown helps speed you through.

I visited my good friend, Paramount Chief Kompa in Masiaka, fifty miles north of the capital. He was receiving a visit from one of the UK ebola monitoring teams led by a British police superintendant who had driven down from Port Loko, still one of the districts of concern alongwith Kono in the north. Chief Kompa outlined some of the problems he continues to face in his Chiefdom which borders the Western area. He related one particularly disturbing incident in one of his villages when after an ebola victim had been buried safely by one of the ebola burial teams, relatives came back at night and dug the body up to perform the traditional rites.

As a result further deaths ensued. He noted the particular problems faced by those who have recovered from ebola when returning to their homes. Not only does the fear of stigmatization persist but they return to nothing, their goods and belongings having been destroyed as part of the quarantine precautions. In his view it would be better to encamp the survivors all together for a while and provide them with food and lodging. Food, he said, was in short supply.

A lady Sierra Leone police officer, who was accompanying the British team, outlined the increasing problems of unsafe sex by returning male ebola survivors who are ignoring the warning to avoid sex for three months or at least use condoms. There have now been several reported cases of women becoming infected in this way. The officer predicted that this could become the prime cause of the continued spread of the deadly disease.

Another group of people who are facing particular problems with the ebola threat are the disabled and especially the blind. The 'no touch' policy is especially difficult for the blind who rely upon touch to 'see'. My work with the blind schools and institutions in the country has forcibly brought this home to me. Government needs to address this problem; a point I made when I called on His Excellency the President.

President Koroma shares the cautious optimism of the experts that the tide is turning and has even predicted that the country will achieve 'zero new cases' by the end of March? He continues to travel widely around the country warning his citizens not to become complacent and to remain vigilant.

Postscript

In the midst of the ebola epidemic the Sierra Leone Government has decided to go ahead and enforce the introduction of a ban on all right-hand drive vehicles, with the threat of fines of up to half a million leones. I have long advocated a ban on right-hand drive poda podas as they disgorge their passengers onto the traffic side of the busy roads. To my mind, banning all vehicles seems excessive and unnecessary, but especially at this time when one would have thought that the police have more important things to do! I am told that some of the ambulances that have been brought into the country to help with the ebola crisis are right-hand drive. Will they be banned too?

Peter Penfold
Former British High Commissioner to Sierra Leone
16 January 2015

Chapter Twenty One

FAITH IN AFRICA

I have always been fascinated by the early African explorers such as Burton and Speke and Livingstone in East and Central Africa or Mungo Park and Heinrich Barth in West Africa. I would have loved to have been around in those times to follow in their rugged footsteps. When I first went to Uganda I had it in mind to retrace the steps of Richard Burton piecemeal at various intervals throughout my three year tour but sadly two coups and constant insecurity prevented me from doing so. I could but marvel at what the early explorers endured and yet, notwithstanding modern equipment and communications, it was sometimes easier to travel around Africa two centuries ago than in today's world.

A bunch of Oxford University students discovered this when they tried to retrace the steps of Mungo Park in West Africa. It was back in the 1980s when I was working in the West African department of the Foreign and Commonwealth Office. The group were stopped at some remote border crossing by some very officious immigration officers. The students refused to pay the exorbitant fees demanded by the avaricious officials to cross the border and as a result they had to retrace their steps and fly back to the UK. Modern day bureaucracy and corruption were more daunting than swollen rivers, wild animals and malaria.

The Victorian explorers were the pop or football stars of their time. The search for example to find the source of the Nile was as great an endeavour as putting a man on the moon. Of course this whole concept of white explorers coming to the continent to 'discover' parts of Africa has rightly been questioned. President Museveni in Uganda had the plaque removed near the town of Jinja which announced that the source of the Nile had been discovered by

John Hanning Speke. As he pointed out the local Africans had always known about it. A reworded plaque was later erected.

Many of the early explorers were, like David Livingstone, missionaries and certainly religion, especially the Christian church played an important role in the development of the African continent. Africans like to tell how the Christian missionaries came to their lands clutching their bibles; they asked the Africans to pray and when they opened their eyes again the Africans held the bibles and the missionaries held the lands! In Uganda there was such a rush by the missionaries to find converts among the African tribes, there were even wars between the Catholics and Anglicans.

But the Christian church, like Islam, has planted deep roots in Africa. I have always felt more comfortable being a Christian in Africa than in the UK. I have gained much from worshipping with my fellow Christians in a wide variety of churches in the countries in which I have served. In the predominantly Moslem north of Nigeria, our Anglican church in Kaduna was not much more that a tinned roofed hut on which the rain would pound in the rainy season and then for part of the year we would go to church clutching our dusters in order to wipe away the dust on the pews from the Harmattan, the dust wind which swept across from the Sahara.

All Saints Cathedral sat atop one of the hills of Kampala just across from the notorious state security offices where Idi Amin's government tortured thousands of poor Ugandans and in the 1970s their cries could be heard during the services. The church was always full when I attended in the mid 1980s. One fought your way out of church against the tide of congregants fighting their way in to find a seat.

The magnificent St Georges' Cathedral in Freetown Sierra Leone was mainly the home of the Krios, the first descendants of the early freed slaves who established Freetown as the capital. The very first CMS (Church Missionary Society) missionaries in Africa came to Freetown and they set the model for the Krios to follow. The liturgy of the Anglican church was strictly adhered to and even in the hot humid climate the congregations came to church in their finest clothes, the ladies in their hats and gloves and the men in their 3 piece striped suits, a mode of dress followed to this day.

Sadly this church, like so many other religious buildings was badly damaged during the rebel invasion of Freetown in 1998. The churches and other religious institutions had played a crucial role in helping bring an end to the 11 year war in Sierra Leone. Thousands took refuge in the mosques and churches during the fighting and it was in these buildings in the eastern end of the city that some of the worst massacres took place. For example sixty six people were murdered in cold blood in the Rogbalan mosque in the suburb of

Kissy and twelve people including children were gunned down in the church of the Brotherhood of the Cross and Star in Wellington.

After the peace agreement had been signed it was the religious leaders in the churches and mosques who preached reconciliation from the pulpits. Given the barbarity of the atrocities committed by the rebels this was not an easy task. On one occasion when the priest had just finished his sermon outlining the Lome Peace Agreement and preaching reconciliation, an elderly lady somewhat hesitantly walked up to the front of the church. She turned embarrassingly to face the congregation and said: 'Please excuse me, I have never done this before, but I feel that I must say something in response to what our priest has just said.'

The packed church went silent as every face turned towards the woman. She went on: 'I am the headmistress of a school. I have been a teacher for thirty years. In all that time, I have been teaching my children about right and wrong, good and bad. If a child is good, he or she is rewarded; if a child is bad or misbehaves, he or she is punished. But now it seems that if a child misbehaves, he should not be punished, he should be rewarded, indeed taking the analogy of the ministerial positions given to the rebels, I should make him a prefect. How can I reverse all that I have been teaching and practising all my life?'

She went back to her pew while the whole congregation sat there stunned. In a simple but very clear way she was voicing the concerns of so many Sierra Leoneans.

But undoubtedly the faiths of the people helped heal the wounds and Sierra Leoneans have enjoyed peace and stability now for many years, as I have witnessed on my many returns to the country.

Sierra Leone in particular has strengthened my Christian faith over the years, but what I have found especially moving is the relationship which exists between the Moslem and Christian communities. Indeed I believe that Sierra Leone sets the example to the world on how Moslems and Christians can live together in peace and harmony, something which the world needs desperately to learn.

There is mutual respect for each other's religion. Though a committed Christian, I have learned so much about the Moslem faith, not particularly from books but especially from my friendship with Alhaji Hussein Jaward. He is the proprietor of the Family Kingdom Resort complex in Freetown – a devout Moslem and shrewd businessman, he is probably the most generous person I have known. One of my guiding tenets from the Bible is the passage from the epistle of James (Ch 2 v 14 and 17):

'What good is it, my brothers, if a man claims to have faith but has no deeds? Can such faith save him?

In the same way, faith by itself, if it is not accompanied by action, is dead.'

In my view Hussein Jaward, a Moslem, exemplifies this, which highlights the similarities between the two religions rather than the differences.

Sierra Leone is a faith based country. 75% of the population regularly attend mosque or church. Inter faith marriages are common. Often within the same family some children may be brought up Christian and others Moslem. Everyone is familiar with each other's prayers and customs. Every meeting starts with Moslem and Christian prayers and if for some reason say a Moslem is not present to say the prayer a Christian will say them on behalf of their Moslem brother.

What Sierra Leoneans cannot understand are people who say that they have no faith. Undoubtedly my faith helped me in my job, especially in Sierra Leone where religious faiths have brought the people together. Within the Moslem faith, unlike elsewhere in the world, there is not the pronounced differences between Shias and Sunnis. When I introduced a visitor to my cook Osman, a devout Moslem, Osman was puzzled to be asked whether he was Sunni or Shia. His reply was 'I am a Moslem'.

Within the Christian faith there are the usual denominations of Anglicans, Catholics, Methodists, etc. In increasing numbers are the Pentecostal and charismatic churches, some of which it must be said are of dubious origins.

The Anglicans are very staunch in their beliefs. Their bishops have found it difficult to accept the direction that the Anglican church has taken in the UK and the West with regards to matters such as homosexual priests, although they more readily accepted female priests. These issues came to the fore within the Anglican church at the turn of the century. The new Archbishop of Canterbury at the time, Dr Rowan Williams, made pronouncements on these issues soon after he was appointed. Shortly afterwards he made a visit to West Africa accompanied by his wife. I was visiting Sierra Leone at the time and as he was to be made a Freeman of the city of Freetown, an honour which already had been bestowed upon me, I became involved in his visit. The climax of the visit programme was a huge gathering at the national football stadium where the Archbishop led prayers for the nation and delivered a thoughtful, reverential homily. He was followed by the Anglican bishop of Freetown, Julius Lynch, who in effect delivered a political speech lambasting the Anglican church in the UK for deserting fundamental Christian teachings.

Dr Williams was clearly taken aback. I advised him at the time that perhaps he should have waited until after his trip to Africa before making public statements about homosexual priests in the UK, and although he may feel that the church had to move forward on these issues, the church in UK should not forget that it was in Africa that the Christian church was growing and expanding, unlike in the UK. If he was shocked by the reception he received in Sierra Leone, he was even more lambasted by the Archbishop of West Africa when he moved on to Ghana from Sierra Leone.

Epilogue

I was 'encouraged' by the Foreign Office to take early retirement in 2002 but this did not stop me maintaining my links with Africa in general and with Sierra Leone in particular. I established a charity for the Milton Margai School for the Blind in Freetown (later extended to cover all six blind schools in Sierra Leone - the UK Association for Schools for the Blind in Sierra Leone). This arose from the tours of the UK we organised by the Freetown blind school choir in 2003 and 2007, when we performed 'My West African Home' in Westminster Abbey (c/f Chapter Nineteen). Later I was approached to become Patron of the Dorothy Springer Trust, the UK registered charity which is helping to provide employment skills, especially IT proficiency, for the disabled in Sierra Leone. This was the brainchild of a dynamic young Sierra Leonean, Dr Abdulai Dumbuya, affectionately known as Abs, who himself was disabled with polio from the age of three and still walks on crutches. Additionally I am a patron of the Hastings Friendship Link, linking Hastings in East Sussex with Hastings on the outskirts of Freetown. I became involved in a rice growing and milling project in Sierra Leone – Lion Mountains Agrico, and, as noted in Chapter Eighteen, I am a Paramount Chief of Sierra Leone.

Early in my retirement I was commissioned to produce various reports including on AIDS in Uganda, UN peacekeeping operations in West Africa, the War Crimes Court in Sierra Leone (in front of which I appeared defending Chief Sam Hinga Norman) and parliamentary democracy in Africa. I published a book, Atrocities, Diamonds and Diplomacy, the Inside Story of the Conflict in Sierra Leone, detailing my time as British High Commissioner and I have also written a couple of children's reading books for primary schools – John-Abu Goes to School and John-Abu Goes to Freetown, written in conjunction with Barbara Davidson, the former administrator of the Milton Margai blind school and published by the Sierra Leonean Writers Series (SLWS). As a result of all these activities I have managed to visit the continent 2/3 times a year which has been very satisfying in keeping up to date with what is going on.

Most of the anecdotes in this collection relate to a bygone age. Times have changed. As a continent Africa still lags behind many other parts of the world in terms of development and stability. When we were struggling to restore President Kabbah's government in Sierra Leone, those of us most closely involved believed, perhaps naively, that we were fighting the cause for the last military coup in Africa; that if another bunch of soldiers decided to take over a democratic government somewhere on the continent, they would face the same reaction from both the people of the country and the international community that the AFRC junta faced in Sierra Leone when the vast majority of the people rejected the military government and the entire international community refused to recognise them. Sadly this was not to be. Shortly afterwards there was a coup in the Ivory Coast and this time the international community led by France resorted again to merely castigating the soldiers and asking when they intended to hold democratic elections. Even as I write this there has been another military coup in Mali. However, compared to the last century, there is generally more stability in Africa with fewer coups and fewer conflicts.

Developmentally there have been immense changes. Probably the most significant change has been in the area of communications, starting with the advent of the mobile phone. When I went off on my drives in Nigeria and Ethiopia or was climbing the Ruwenzori mountains in Uganda, (Chapters One, Two and Fourteen), I was totally cut off from the rest of the world. Even at the end of the last century when I drove down to Bo, the second city of Sierra Leone, I was out of touch with the capital Freetown. It was a great thrill for me on one of my subsequent visits to Sierra Leone to surprise my wife by ringing her back in the UK from Bo. The mobile phone has transformed Africa and not just for talking to one another. For example it was Kenya that led the way in using the mobile phone to make money transfers and now one can even receive a medical prognosis from a qualified doctor over one's mobile phone.

Today laptops and smart phones are everywhere with the obvious changes they bring especially in the fields of education and business. One of my personal projects as High Commissioner in Sierra Leone was to acquire and distribute wind-up radios to every one of the 149 Paramount Chiefs. I contacted the inventor Trevor Baylis to let him know of what enormous benefit his invention had been in Africa. The only limitation for listening to the BBC

World Service on the radios (c/f Chapter Six) had been the limited reach of the radio frequencies. With the spread of satellite communications and the expansion of solar-powered technology wind-up radios are considered old-fashioned. Now any child in the remotest African village can browse the websites and google the answers to any questions!

Some things have not changed. Even some leaders have remained. Yoweri Museveni, who came to power in 1986 when I was in Uganda, is still the President I remember vividly standing on the steps of the Parliament Building in Kampala as Museveni, dressed in his military fatigues was sworn in as President by Sir Peter Allen the British born Chief Justice of Uganda, who was dressed in his full scarlet robes and full judicial wig. Peter had bravely informed Museveni that even though he had claimed over the radio that he was now the President of Uganda, having driven out the Okello regime, he was not legally so until he had been properly sworn in by him, the Chief Justice. Museveni, to his credit, said alright, come and swear me in, and thus I witnessed probably one of the most bizarre sights of post-colonial Africa – a photograph of which can be seen in Peter Allen's book 'Days of Judgement – A Judge in Idi Amin's Uganda'.

Of late it has become fashionable to criticise and discredit Britain's colonial legacy. This is regrettable. All I can say is that in all my experiences in Africa, the number of times I have been attacked or criticised for Britain's colonial heritage were very few. Many of the older Africans with whom I met and worked often lamented the passing of the old colonial days (c/f Chapter Thirteen). There was an efficiency and an impartiality in the colonial times, especially in the areas of administration, education and the judiciary, which gradually became eroded after independence. For example a late friend of mine who had been a colonial district officer in Uganda noted how in his time in the eastern province of Karamoja there were just three British administrators responsible for running the province; when I served in Uganda in the 1980s there were eighty Ugandan civil servants doing the same. Many Sierra Leoneans objected to being forced into independence which, they said, ushered in the demise of the country's once-rich economy. On independence Sierra Leone was richer and more developed than most other newly emerging independent countries like Singapore and Malaysia. When I served there in the 1990s it was officially the poorest country in the world!

When Museveni arrived in the capital Kampala in January 1986, he had with him a number of Rwandese fighters, including one, Paul Kagame, who was appointed head of security intelligence. At that time I was going out with Heidi from the German Embassy and Kagame lived in a house on a compound next door to her. On my visits to Heidi I would exchange greetings with Kagame and his fellow Rwandans as they sat on their verandah swigging their bottles of beer. At the time I never imagined that he would go on to become President of Rwanda and remain so until this day?

They say power corrupts and certainly the practice of clinging on to power still persists in Africa. Take the example of Robert Mugabe (c/f Chapter Nine). He clung onto power in Zimbabwe for so long that he totally ruined this once thriving economy. Regrettably the fine examples of presidents like Mandela in South Africa, Senghor in Senegal, Mogae in Botswana and Kabbah in Sierra Leone who voluntarily stood down at the end of their tenures as heads of state are rare.

Many of the conflicts in Africa in the second half of the last century were exacerbated and sometimes even encouraged by the Cold War. When I went to Ethiopia in 1975 the country was very much in the Western camp under Emperor Haile Selassie and across the border Somalia was considered a Soviet satellite under President Siad Barre. With Mengistu coming to power the position reversed. Ethiopia became pro Soviet and Somalia pro the West. The break-up of the Soviet Union and the collapse of the Berlin Wall brought an end to many of the conflicts. There is still a competition between outside powers to gain influence in Africa for commercial or political gain but today it is China which is by far the most dominant and aggressive.

The magic of Africa which first enticed me fifty years ago is still there. On my frequent visits I remain enthralled with the African dawn as the sun rises and the sun-baked earth comes to life, and with the sky at night when the dazzling stars are so bright you can almost reach out and touch them. The marvellous sights of the Murchison Falls (Chapter Twelve) and the snow-capped Ruwenzori Mountains (Chapter Fourteen) remain, although with global warming how much longer will that be?

And what of the Africans themselves? In this collection of anecdotes I have tried to recapture the magic of living and working in Africa. Like in all societies there are good and bad, but generally there is a common decency and good naturedness in the African. He, and especially she, works hard to survive, often with little reward.

Africa is still a place where one can make a difference if one is prepared to try, albeit in a small way.

Take the example of Simon Ssekankya. Simon was the son of Daisy one of my three domestic staff in Kampala. The other two members of my 'extended Ugandan family' were Charles and Joyce (c/f Chapter Fifteen). As a baby toddler Simon cheerily wandered around our compound at 35, Prince Charles Drive in the Kololo suburb of Kampala while his mother worked in the house. A few years later after I had left Uganda, Jim Atkinson, the then incumbent Deputy High Commissioner, wrote to say that sadly Daisy had died from the rampant spread of AIDS in the country leaving behind Simon and his two younger sisters. We set up a trust fund to look after the three of them. Simon worked hard and gained a place at the prestigious Makerere University. After graduation I was able to help him get a job with one of the banks in Kampala.

On a subsequent visit to Uganda Simon proudly took me, and Charles and Joyce, for a ride in his first car, a rickety old banger. He mentioned that the job with the bank was going well but to help make ends meet he was also selling sand and cement. A couple of years went by and I was commissioned to write a report on AIDs in Uganda. I contacted Simon from the UK before travelling. He said he would pick me up from the airport. He also mentioned somewhat ominously that he had given up the job at the bank to focus on selling the sand and cement. There was Simon on my arrival at Entebbe airport, looking very smart. We went out to the car park and I am looking for the rickety old car when Simon leads me to the latest model Mercedes Benz and we get in. The next day he picks me up again from my hotel in the Mercedes to show me, he says, his new business. We drive to the industrial area and there is Hardware World, the biggest hardware factory in the country. Simon is now the 'Mr B&Q' of Uganda, and among his many employees are Charles and Joyce. His success is undoubtedly down to his own efforts and hard work but the story does show just how much can be achieved in the face of adversity with a little helping hand.

And then there's Osman Kamara in Sierra Leone. Osman at 11 years of age was the youngest member of the Blind School choir which we took to the UK in 2003. When Abs Dumbuya started the computer training courses at the Dorothy Springer Trust in Freetown I arranged for some of our blind children to also receive the IT training by acquiring the computer software which enables blind people to use computers. Osman took to it like the proverbial duck to water so much so that he is now one of DST's instructors; in other words here is a blind person teaching sighted people how to use a computer. How about that?!

So many friends and colleagues can recite similar examples of the diligence and determination to succeed with just that little help. This is what I have found so satisfying through all these years of my association with Africa. For me it has been a two way street. I have benefited enormously from the help of so many of my African friends and colleagues. My faith has been strengthened; my life has been enriched and exciting.

Thank you.